Karsten "Ted" Aschenbrandt/Rudolf Jaeger

THE BIG
SMOKER BOOK

Barbecue Techniques and Recipes

Schiffer Publishing Ltd®

4880 Lower Valley Road • Atglen, PA 19310

THE BIG SMOKER BOOK

Barbecue Techniques and Recipes

Karsten "Ted" Aschenbrandt/Rudolf Jaeger

Schiffer Publishing Ltd
4880 Lower Valley Road • Atglen, PA 19310

Grillsportverein
[Grilling Sports Club]

Other Schiffer Books by the Author:
The Perfect Sausage: Making and Preparing Homemade Sausage.
  Karsten "Ted" Aschenbrandt. ISBN: 978-0-7643-4302-5.
  $19.99
Other Schiffer Books on Related Subjects:
Dutch Oven: Cast-Iron Cooking Over an Open Fire. Carsten Bothe.
  ISBN: 978-0-7643-4218-9. $29.99
Pure BBQ. Steffen Eichhorn, Stefan Marquard, and Stephan
  Otto. ISBN: 978-0-7643-4013-0. $24.99

Library of Congress Control Number: 2012954932

Originally published by: Heel Verlag GmbH as *Das Grosse Smoker-Buch: Grilltechniken & Rezepte* in 2010
Text: Karsten "Ted" Aschenbrandt, Rudolf Jaeger
All Photos: WINK PHOTOGRAPHER GmbH, Ramon Wink, www.winkphotographer.com
*(**With the exception of** Archive: p. 16; Library of Congress, USA: p. 17, 18, 19; Thosa Trade: p. 22; Rudolf Jaeger: p. 31 (box), 54 (inset); Stockfood: p. 52; Fotolia: p. 112 (© Stocksnapper), 120 (© davidphotos))*
Graphics: Claudia Renierkens, renierkens kommunikationsdesign, Cologne
Editing: Petra Hundacker, Christine Birnbaum
Translator: Christine Marie Elliston

Designed by Mark David Bowyer
Type set in ATTorino / Stone Sans

ISBN: 978-0-7643-4328-5

- No responsibility is accepted for the correctness of this information. -

Printed in China

Schiffer Books are available at special discounts for bulk purchases for sales promotions or premiums. Special editions, including personalized covers, corporate imprints, and excerpts can be created in large quantities for special needs. For more information contact the publisher.

Published by Schiffer Publishing, Ltd.
4880 Lower Valley Road
Atglen, PA 19310
Phone: (610) 593-1777; Fax: (610) 593-2002
E-mail: Info@schifferbooks.com

For the largest selection of fine reference books on this and related subjects, please visit our website at
www.schifferbooks.com.
You may also write for a free catalog.

This book may be purchased from the publisher.
Please try your bookstore first.

We are always looking for people to write books on new and related subjects. If you have an idea for a book, please contact us at
proposals@schifferbooks.com

In Europe, Schiffer books are distributed by
Bushwood Books
6 Marksbury Ave.
Kew Gardens
Surrey TW9 4JF England
Phone: 44 (0) 20 8392 8585; Fax: 44 (0) 20 8392 9876
E-mail: info@bushwoodbooks.co.uk
Website: www.bushwoodbooks.co.uk

Dedication

We dedicate this book to the numerous BBQ and smoker fans and friends in the world who unremittingly collected, improved, and gladly shared recipes. Without this committed community and its solidarity, it would not have been at all possible to create so many different, delicious dishes.

Smoking doesn't only mean eating, but rather finding friends, exchanging ideas, and enjoying some quality of life.

Welcome to our (and now hopefully also your) BBQ world!

Contents

Farmer FG 70

Joe's Smoker Chuckwagon 16"

Farmer FG 40

Bos Food Smoker 24"

Weber Smokey Mountain

Apollo Water Smoker

Weber Performer

Louisiana CS 450

Big Green Egg

PART 2: THE DISHES

Contents

Hot dogs and hamburgers—until a few years ago this was inextricably linked with the idea of grilling. Fortunately today we are light years away from this perception, and grilling is enjoying growing popularity. A reason for this rising popularity is certainly the fact that grilling is an immensely communicative type of food preparation.

It is no wonder that smoking is also finding greater appeal. This low-temperature cooking method has already been practiced in the States for hundreds of years and is increasingly exciting grilling fans in "Old Europe." Whoever enjoys the outstanding taste of "low and slow" will certainly be on the lookout for the right places in their backyards for a smoker as quickly as possible.

The manufacturers of grills and smokers have met the growing demand by expanding their array of products. Thus, now a variety of smokers in different price ranges are available— of course with a corresponding selection of accessories.

The special wishes of smoker fans are also no longer as strange to meat suppliers and butcher shops. More and more often people are getting unusual cuts of meat that are especially suitable for smoking.

Our enthusiasm for smoking goes back to the time in which it was still a niche topic. We are familiar with all facets of smoking and grilling and are excited to be able to make available to you the knowledge we have gained over the years.

We wish you leisure time, good company, knowledgeable guests, and naturally great enjoyment when smoking our recipes.

Karsten "Ted" Aschenbrandt and Rudolf Jaeger
Summer 2010

Part 1
THE SMOKER

- A Brief History of Barbecue
- Smoker—A Small Study of Equipment and Tips for Maintenance
- Fuel
- Accessories

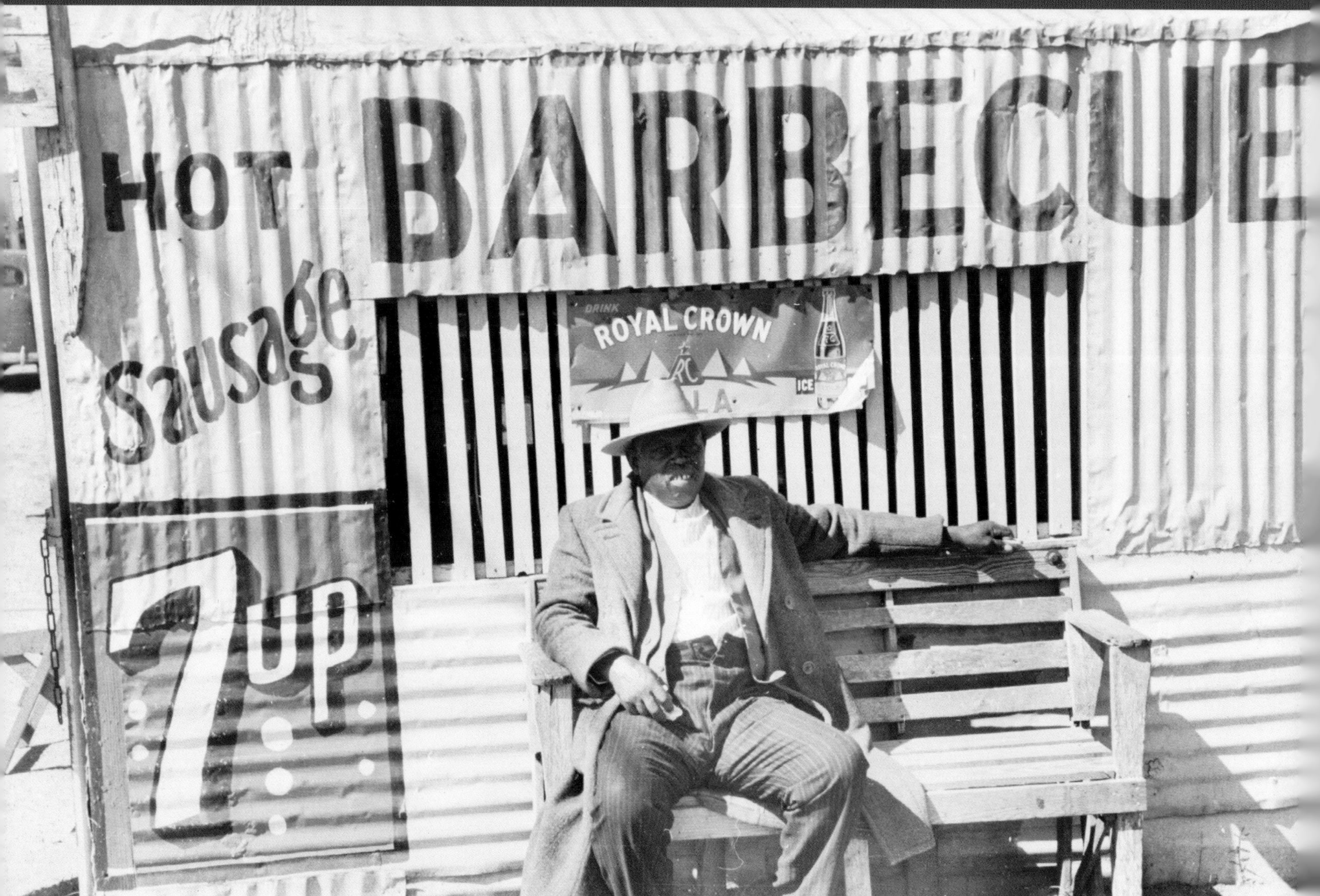
HOT
BARBECUE
Sausages
DRINK
ROYAL CROWN
RC
ICE
7up

A BRIEF
HISTORY
OF BARBECUE

It sizzles and crackles. The smell of juicy meat fills the air, stories and jokes are told in good company. A long time ago barbecue and with it the increasingly popular smokers have found their way into our area and with them a new era of friendliness and good food.

Barbecuing and Grilling Are Two Completely Different Things

Barbecue is often used as a synonym for grilling. However, the essential difference is in the cooking method. While grilling meat consists of very small pieces and is cooked over heat at a temperature of approximately 390° Fahrenheit to 570° Fahrenheit [200°C to 300°C], considerably larger pieces of meat (in some cases even entire animals) are cooked by hot smoke at a temperature between 190° Fahrenheit and 320° Fahrenheit [90°C and 160°C] when barbecuing. Thus, it is possible that a piece of meat can take up to twenty hours until it is done.

Barbecue—or simply BBQ—and smoking are inextricably linked with each other. But where does the term "barbecue" come from and what does it mean exactly?

Viva la Barbecue – So It Began

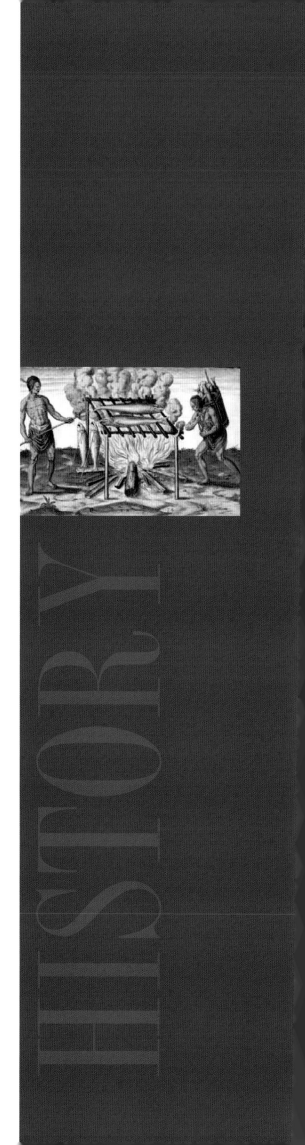

The exact origin of the term "barbecue" is not clear. According to one theory, the oldest records that deal with the term "barbecue" go back to the early fifteenth century and stem from Spanish explorers who traveled the Caribbean. They observed and documented the indigenous peoples cooking meat, which was done on a framework made of sticks over and next to an open fire. This special cooking method was already known in the Caribbean and along the entire mainland coast to Brazil during the time of the conquest of America. The indigenous peoples used agave and banana leaves that they wrapped around the meat, thus achieving an exotic flavor. After cooking, the fat was used as soup for an appetizer. The Spaniards were involved in the continued development of BBQ, as they established pork in America. Pork's BBQ cult status continues to today. Before the arrival of pork, the indigenous peoples used primarily reptiles (especially snakes), fish, rodents, and birds. The natives called the wooden construction "*barbacòa*," which subsequently developed quickly into a well-known saying. The term "barbecue" was first officially named in the *Oxford English Dictionary* in 1661, in which it is first described only as the wooden framework, and later as the meal.

The first documented usage of the term "barbecue" coincides with the mention in the *Oxford English Dictionary*. The following sentence is found in Edmund Hickeringill's work, *Jamaica Viewed*:

"Animals are slain, And their flesh forthwith Barbacu'd and eat."

Barbecue as Presidents' Food

In 1733, Benjamin Lynde and also later the American presidents George Washington and Thomas Jefferson used the term barbecue to describe their traditional festivities. The BBQ as a victory celebration was popular among the American leaders for many decades. In 1923 Jack C. Walton, governor of the state of Oklahoma, hosted an opulent BBQ with 289 cattle, 70 pigs, 36 sheep, 2540 rabbits, 134 opossums, 15 deer, 1427 chickens, and 1 antelope.

According to another theory barbecue is derived from the French expression, *barbe à queue*, which means "from the beard to the tail" and describes the cooking

of entire animals. Another possible explanation of the origin of the word combines the English and French definition. In 1829 the *National Intelligencer* labeled President Andrew Jackson's followers as "Barbacus" because they were loyally devoted to their leader and did all the very best to support him and provide him with a happy life. In English there is an expression for this type of readiness to make sacrifices that is not found in other languages: "Going the whole hog, from the beard (barbe) to the tail (queue)."

From this moment on, the term barbecue has frequently appeared in the most diverse settings of world history. The meaning is always the same: cooking meat or other food at low to medium heat.

Whichever origin story you believe and whether you prefer the written-out barbecue, the abbreviation BBQ, or the minimalist term Q for the whole thing, fortunately has no influence on the outcome, and it lies only in the eye of the beholder.

Pig Pits

BBQ celebrated its big breakthrough around 1800 at the time of plantations in the South. Every day many people were busy with hard work and had to be fed as easily as possible, with little expense. Thus, slow and less labor-intensive cooking became more widespread. The main ingredient for this most classic form of BBQ was pork. Pigs are easy to breed, eat everything, and are very nutritious from their fat. These animals are still popular at BBQs today.

It's All in the Technique

The original BBQ technique is different from the subsequently popular wooden constructions. The great amount of work and the high danger of fire called for a transformation. First, a pit was dug. In this approximately 3 feet [1 meter] wide and 1.6 feet [half-meter] deep pit in the ground (the length was determined by the number of eaters), a wood fire was started and burnt down until an even firebed was made. The pigs, gutted and splayed out, were stretched out on sticks and slats and placed over the pit. A pit master ensured a heat that was well distributed and not too hot by putting more wood on the fire.

Thus, it was absolutely possible, save the preparations, to cook fifteen to twenty pigs with only one person. After sixteen to twenty hours over a low temperature, the meat was so tender that you could easily pick it from the bone. Cutting up the meat was unnecessary. With a sauce, mostly vinegar or water based, you had enough meat to feed workers and slaves.

Moving into Private Gardens

Quite a few people enjoy this type of eating and practice it at home. They meet in the evening in their own garden or in a field. Thus, the first "pig pits" moved into private households of southerners. Here the followers of the delicious barbecue method proved to be quite creative. If their own garden was too small for a large hole, a tub would have to serve.

Made in Germany

Even if the origin of the term BBQ cannot be clearly geographically assigned, we know who carried out the pioneering work for the spreading and refinement of BBQ: emigrants with German roots.

Because the first people who sold the necessary meat for barbecuing inevitably opened businesses and had to pay taxes, names of these BBQ pioneers are famous. Among others, they include George Ridenhour, Sid Weaver, Warner Stamey, Jess Swicegood, and John Blackwelder. These surnames were originally Reitnaur, Weber, Stemme, Schweissgauth, and Schwarzwälder in the Old World and thus refer to families of German descent.

Particularly in all German-speaking countries, pork was considered a meat for the working class. Because most immigrants in America belonged to this class, they were most familiar with its preparation and passed their sound knowledge on to further generations. For the butchers among German immigrants and their heirs, brining meat was as routine as smoking—ideal qualifications for the enhancement and perfection of the "traditional" barbecue.

Over time national specialties were created. In the meantime, the shoulder was considered the best cut for pulled pork. Its fat is succulent and ensures a very good absorption of the smoky flavor. The German butchers then took, from their perspective, the best piece and prepared it according to the method characteristic of their country. The right mix of the old German art of butchering and the traditional hog-cooking culture of the southern states provided the basis for today's BBQ.

Piedmont Style:
Barbecue Is a Big Seller

At the beginning of the twentieth century, the first BBQ kiosks shot up like mushrooms in the mountains of the Piedmont region, specifically Lexington and Salisbury. At these small stands, the meat was both traditionally sold on a plate or as a sandwich. The owners first mixed ketchup in traditional vinegar sauce and took only individual cuts from the pig, exactly like their German forerunners. The finished meat was served sliced, pulled, or chopped.

The first professional barbecue restaurant dates to 1920. Warner Stamey opened his establishment in Lexington, North Carolina, and from the beginning appeared keen on experimenting. Thus, for example, another specialty of the southern states was created: small, deep-fried balls of dough called hushpuppies, on solid barbecue meat.

The restaurants that quickly continued to spread certainly did not replace snack stands. To the contrary: with the invention of the automobile small stands were established on the roadside: barbecue "to go" became at least as popular as the classic hot dog. In 1921, J. G. Kirby founded the "Pig Stands Company" that operated over 100 barbecue stands, especially in the south and southwest. However, with the increase of large international fast food chains, the first period of prosperity for BBQ came to an end decades later.

The Typical Barbecue Restaurant Is...

The end of the barbecue stands in the southern states did not mean the end of the numerous barbecue restaurants. With the exception of Memphis and Kansas City, they are primarily located in rural areas today. Given strong regional differences, the restaurants have a unique character, both in terms of ingredients and preparation. This occasionally has a chaotic effect. In her work *American Material Culture*, Edith Mayo describes such a typical barbecue restaurant as follows:

"These are often barbecue eateries identified by torn screen doors, scratched and dented furniture, cough syrup calendars, potato chip racks, sometimes a jukebox, and always a counter, producing an ambience similar to a country-line beer joint."

Smoker Around the World

Small Amounts Allow Flexibility and Mobility

For a classic, traditional southern barbecue an entire animal and a large hole in the ground are required. With a technique that uses cuts of meat, smaller pieces are prepared and consumed. A smaller piece of meat, such as a shoulder or neck up to eleven pounds [five kilograms], can also be very well prepared in a small device—the smoker. It is not clear who invented it. Roughly 3,000 years ago the Chinese were already cooking with smoke and at low temperatures. Certainly, however, the popularity of this cooking method was introduced by the colonization of North America and from there set forth on its triumphal procession around the world.

Once they had spread to different regions of the United States, the smokers were gradually provided with regional products. Thus, for example, in Texas cuts of beef found their way into the smoke.

Brisket and tough meat for soup have proven to be perfect for the smoker and are integral components in the long list of recipes. Next to brisket, pork shoulder, and pork neck, ribs are the fourth largest pillar of classic BBQ. Poultry and other types of meats were experimented with, and now there are hardly any ingredients that can't be smoked—anywhere in the world!

SMOKER –

A SMALL STUDY OF EQUIPMENT AND TIPS FOR MAINTENANCE

You would like to think that a completely normal oven is sufficient to cook meat at a low temperature. In principle that is correct, but when smoke comes into play, the oven reaches it limits. For this, you need a device that generates smoke, stays outdoors, and functions reliably regardless of the weather.

A smoker does just that. Its appearance is dependent on the model, but the principle of operation is always the same: A dry heat is produced separately from the food and is evenly distributed. In this heat, enriched with smoke formed from burning wood, the meat is cooked over a long period of time at temperatures around 230° Fahrenheit [110°C] and becomes wonderfully tender and juicy. Where the heat is produced, how the air flows, and which fuel is used depends on the type of smoker.

The range of available smokers is steadily becoming more extensive, and, thus, it is no problem for all tastes and budgets to find the right device. There are many smoker fans who know a lot about metal construction and therefore build their smokers themselves. It saves money and the result has a very personal touch.

The Most Important Smoker Models

Offset or Barrel Smoker

In recent years more and more offset smokers have come onto the market. There are two terms for this type of smoker. "Offset smoker" means that the combustion chamber in which a wood fire produces the heat is offset to the cooking chamber, the "pit." The correct name for this combustion chamber is the "side firebox." It doesn't matter if it is located to the right, left, center, or underneath. The name "barrel smoker" refers to the cylindrical shape of this type of smoker that is often made from a pipe. Certainly the most important feature is that this smoker has separated chambers.

In addition to the classic thick-walled offset smokers that have a wall thickness of .15" [4 mm] or more, very inexpensive new models are offered today that are made out of substantially thinner metal. However, they do not have the quality and heat retention capacity of their clearly massive prototypes, are thus short-lived, and are sensitive to weather effects. Barrel smokers mostly have two wheels and two legs and, depending on their weight, are moved with more or less effort.

In contrast, smokers manufactured for catering are frequently mounted onto automobile trailers. This allows for the mobility necessary for use outside of the home. This range of models includes equipment with and without cooking towers and weight classes from under 220 pounds [100 kilograms] to over one ton. Whoever owns a sufficiently large backyard can also build a unique BBQ locomotive with a coal car, dining car, and the appropriate rails. The trend of building such offset smokers yourself continues, and in diverse barbecue forums worldwide you can admire many self-made constructions.

The functionality of the smoker is simple and effective. The heat that is produced by the fire in the side firebox—the combustion chamber that is offset on the side—and the smoke escape through the cooking chamber—the pit—and are evenly distributed around the food. To have a more subtle smoky flavor, the lid of the side firebox can be slightly opened so that a portion of the smoke can escape directly upwards and correspondingly less smoke flows into the cooking chamber.

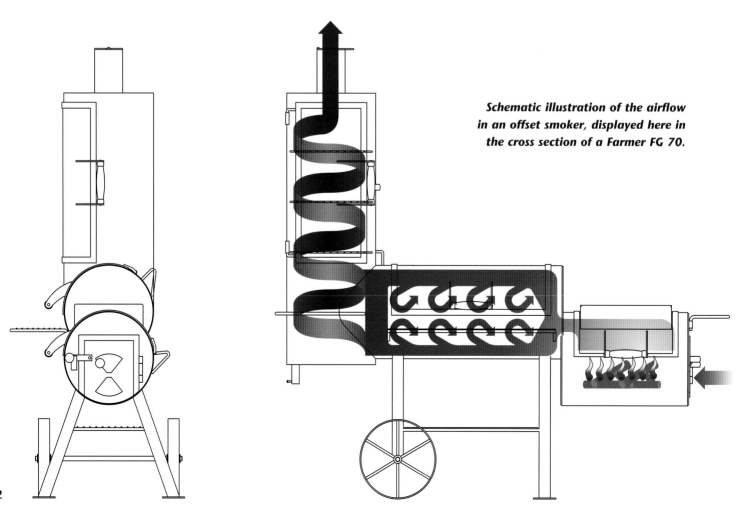

Schematic illustration of the airflow in an offset smoker, displayed here in the cross section of a Farmer FG 70.

and Their Features

In addition to the barbecue introduced here in the book, a smoker can be used at higher temperatures for baking, braising, or roasting. The temperature is mainly controlled by the size of the fire and the position of the inlet dampers on the side firebox. The general rule is that a big fire with a lot of air results in a large amount of heat, while a small one produces less. The heavy weight of many offset smokers results from the large wall thickness of the steel pipes that are used. The thickness of the steel and also the associated mass of these smokers are decisive factors for wind sensitivity, fluctuations in temperature, and heat retention. They provide for the necessary heat buffer, and only due to its mass is it possible to keep such a large smoker at a constant temperature with little fuel.

Models like the Farmer FG 70 and Joe's Smoker Chuckwagon are well suited for the food service industry due to their very large grilling area of over 3' [1m] in length in the cooking chamber. With a material thickness of over .19" [5 mm], smokers equipped with a smoking tower weigh over 440 pounds [200 kilograms].

Farmer FG 70

Joe's Smoker Chuckwagon 16"

Convection plate for better heat distribution in the smoker

The smoker tower as a warming surface

The cooking tower can also very well be used for smoking and warming, an advantage not to be underestimated with larger BBQs. Swivel arms can also be attached over the side firebox for hanging cast iron pots. The grates in the cooking chamber are often made of thick stainless steel bars, and by means of special hot plate inserts, from the Rumo company for example, the cooking chamber can be upgraded for the use of pots and pans. With a pit length of over 31" [80 cm] the use of a heat conducting pipe in the cooking chamber is highly recommended. With this, the heat and smoke are evenly distributed to the other end.

On the lids of the side fireboxes there are often hot plates welded on—pots and pans can be placed here as needed. From the burning fire underneath, the right heat is produced for frying or cooking. For domestic use, smaller smokers without a smoking tower with smaller grilling surfaces, such as, for example, the FG 40 from Farmer, are well suited. With this model you can host approximately ten people. Despite the purchase price, you gain a lot when you consider that the life of a smoker is many decades. Another advantage of this smoker is the fact that you can still move it easily in the yard or on the patio, and it does not need as much space as the larger models. Premium manufacturers have models with rubber wheels, and special smoker mats are available commercially.

Bos Food Smoker 24"

Farmer FG 40

It does not matter which model you choose, but it is important to look for to cleanly welded seams and a tightly closing lid. The parts subject to wear on the smoker are the charcoal grates and the handles that are often made of wood, which are easy to replace. Depending on weather conditions, hardwood handles hold up longer than softwood handles—metal coil springs are a long-lasting solution. However, they have to be specially manufactured by a metal worker. With an additional side work table you can extend the shelf space, but most models already have a shelf in front of the pit.

One can justifiably call the Bos Food Smoker 24" an XXXL-Smoker. With a weight of over one ton, it is the heavyweight among models made by hand in Germany. It is equipped with three built-in thermometers, a pit with a double damper system, and a counterweight, and is suited for BBQs with several hundred guests.

If there is a hurry or hunger has set in early at a BBQ, the grate of the side firebox is ideal as a direct grill for steaks, burgers, or sausages. In the recipes section there is a collection of such *entremets* in the chapter *Snacks* starting on page 124.

Steaks from
the side firebox

Water or Bullet Smoker

For a cost-effective entrance into the world of smoking, so-called water or bullet smokers are suitable due to their low weight and space requirement. These smokers are characterized by the use of only one chamber and a thin exterior wall made of steel. Heat generation, heat buffer, aeration, de-aeration, and finally the cooked food is all found under one lid. With these models, the necessary heat is produced with briquettes in a charcoal basket. Over this there is a pan that is filled with water and serves to retain heat. This pan gives the water smoker its name, but it can also be filled with sand, gravel, or stones, which can save you from refilling the water. The name "bullet smoker" refers to the shape of the smoker, which is sometimes reminiscent of a bullet. With the help of heat storage by water or stones an even heat can be maintained over many hours without a problem. Therefore, this smoker is optimally suited for BBQs that continue over night. Water smokers run up to 25 hours without maintenance or refueling.

If stone, gravel, or sand is used as an alternative to water, it must carefully be covered with aluminum foil due to the dripping fat. The doors serve to refill water and fuel and to measure the temperature of the food.

Between the water pan and the interior wall in all bullet smokers there is only a small, circular opening that lets out the heat and smoke upwards. The direct heat of the briquettes, with which a water smoker is normally powered, is thereby shielded. The air circulation can be regulated by the ventilation openings on the lid and under the charcoal. The further the vents are opened, the more oxygen hits the flames, and the more the temperature climbs in the smoker. The grate sits over the water pan, on which the food is placed. Usually there is another grill grate above it by which the capacity of the smoker doubles.

In the lid there is often a rail on which fish hooks can be hung, which makes this smoker also attractive for fishermen.

Barbecue Smoker

Weber Smokey Mountain

Some water smoker models have a stack system that makes a smoker versatile with a modular design. The lower hemisphere can also be used as a normal kettle grill for direct or indirect grilling. The water pan, to retain heat, and the lower grate are built in the next stack module. In the following modules there is only one grate each. With up to three modules you can adjust the surface as necessary.

The Weber Smokey Mountain Cooker and the Napoleon Apollo have been established as reliable and stable equipment.

Water smoker with stacks (module with buckles)

The interior of a water smoker with two grate levels

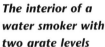

The Apollo water smoker

The Minion Method

Jim Minion's heating method for water smokers is especially interesting and effective. It is particularly suited for long BBQs that range over 6 to 20 hours. This method is particularly useful for the overnight BBQ. The setup for the Minion Method is quick and easy, and a constant temperature will be reached that can be maintained over a long period of time.

1 The briquettes are best placed around an empty can, which can carefully be removed afterwards, located in the center of the charcoal grate. The live charcoal will be placed in this free space later.

2 Now woodchips can be distributed over the briquettes. They produce the smoke that would be absent with only a charcoal fire.

3 Now the lit briquettes are carefully placed into the hole (can) in the center. The hole should be filled evenly; to measure the amount of briquettes you can use the empty can.

4 The lit briquettes now evenly work outwards over many hours and gradually burn the woodchips.

5 The next level, the water pan, is placed on top. Here marble gravel is used to retain heat.

6 To protect the gravel from dripping fat cover it with aluminum foil.

7 The food can now be placed on the grate.

Kettle Grill as a Smoker

Even Weber kettle grills with 22" and 26" [57 and 67 cm] diameters can be used, with the help of the so-called "Smokenator," as small, functional smokers. The stainless steel insert is simply attached to the side in the kettle grill, and thereby it is locked in place in the charcoal grate and two of the four grill grate mountings. On the top side there are two holes for combustion, which allow the heat and smoke to flow into the kettle, and a water pan. If this pan is filled, the water inside begins to cook. This energy does not heat up the kettle but rather is absorbed by the water. The result is that the kettle runs on low temperature, which is essential during smoking.

Smokenator insert for Weber kettle grills

Weber Performer

Wood Pellet Smoker

Control box with pellet filling.

In their countries of origin, Canada and the United States, pellet smokers have long been widespread, while in Europe they are relatively new or unknown. The wood pellets, made from wood shavings, and used as fuel, are especially environmentally friendly and also available at a relatively low cost almost everywhere because of the popularity of wood pellet heating. However, for pellet smokers only hardwoods can be used. The manufacturers of pellet smokers offer different, special BBQ flavor pellets from hickory, mesquite, cherry tree, and many other types of wood for the required smoky flavor. The special attraction to these smokers lies in the independently running heating for over eight hours depending on the pellet storage bin.

Louisiana CS 450

There is no need to constantly add firewood, and the smoker functions almost by itself due to the use of an auger. Here the archaic use of wood and fire is left up to a machine—it's a matter of taste. The constantly running fan in the control box ensures a consistent aeration of the cooking chamber and provides the flames with oxygen. Compared to their thick-walled colleagues, steel pellet smokers are low in weight and require only a small storage space. As a result they can be used in the smallest space, such as a balcony, and are easy to transport. However, the disadvantage is the dependency on electricity and also the running sound of the fan. However, there should soon be 12 volt battery-powered versions. The wattage of pellet smokers is very minor and amounts to approximately 45 watts/hour.

A pellet smoker is suited for smoking, BBQ, and grilling. It is easily adjusted to the desired temperature with the controller. It only takes approximately 15 minutes to heat up and is similar to the quick initial start of a gas grill. Small pellet smokers are suited for families, while for larger parties or restaurant use pellet smokers are available with over 3 square feet [1 square meter] of grilling surface.

Igniter rod   **Auger in the burn pot**

Ceramic Smoker

Over 3,000 years ago the Chinese built the first ceramic ovens. The Japanese copied them and called these ceramic grills "*kamado*" which loosely translated means fireplace or furnace. In the Second World War American soldiers brought these *kamados* with them from Japan into the United States. Their versatility quickly appealed to numerous barbecue fans there. These thick-walled ceramic eggs have also been available in Europe for several years. Big Green Egg, Monolith, and Kamado established themselves as brands. What is special about them is the even heat distribution that is produced in the interior and the minor fuel requirement at a constant temperature over many hours, which is a special advantage during smoking. The temperatures range from 122° Fahrenheit to 572° Fahrenheit [50°C to 400°C], which is achieved after a few minutes in the most heat-resistant ceramic. A ceramic grill can be used as a smoker, baking oven, or grill: even the preparation of pizza at a high temperature is no problem. Smoking in a ceramic oven is easy: the slide control on the bottom and the air regulation allow a precise temperature setting.

Big Green Egg with a practical wooden frame

Smoker Maintenance

Maintaining a smoker requires minimal effort. On the inside of the lid a smoke patina forms from use, which is comparable to the build-up in a teapot that also should not be removed. This is also the reason why smokers are not painted on the inside. For cleaning the cooking chamber and the grill grates a wire brush and hot water are sufficient. Heavy, environmentally hazardous cleaners are only advisable in very rare cases. For more difficult incrustations, a grill and oven cleaner helps. The cooking chamber and side firebox can be cleaned with a garden hose. To remove fat residue, hot water and dish soap are helpful. Then the opened cooking chamber can be dried out.

Because smokers can stay outside all year round it is only a matter of time before the first rust spots appear. Putting covers over them normally accelerates the process because most are air impermeable and often collect condensation water underneath the cover. Smokers with a reasonable material thickness of .19″ [5 mm] or more are sufficiently protected from rusting through because of their thickness, and the accumulating rust is more of a visual problem. The rust spots are quickly removed with a wire brush and you can spray the spot afterwards with heat-resistant enamel (oven enamel). Then the applied color is baked at a low temperature; a temperature that is too high will burn the enamel.

A self-made linseed oil-graphite-turpentine substitute mixture is an alternative, but is time-consuming to make and cumbersome to apply. Additionally, the result compared to the spray is often not as good, therefore, the spray is clearly recommended here.

The handles that are often made of wood certainly require the most maintenance. Coil spring handles are a lifelong solution here. The side firebox should always be cleaned of the remaining salty ashes after smoking to prevent corrosion on the inside.

The small bucket under the cooking chamber, affixed to a drain and used for dripping fat, can simply be rinsed—and then the smoker is ready for the next barbecue.

Smoker bucket on the drain

Rust does not limit functionality,...

but it is not easy on the eyes.

Here manual work is necessary.

Before...

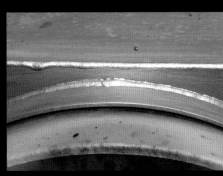

...after.

Sprayed with heat-resistant oven enamel, the smoker quickly looks good again.

FUEL

Smoke is not just smoke, even if it initially appears as such, because aside from wood and fire nothing else belongs.

Wood

For heating up a smoker, well-dried wood is the first choice. The wood should be untreated and dried for two to three years. The cross section of the piece of wood should amount to 2" to 2.3" [5 to 6 cm], and a length of approximately 10" [25 cm] should not be exceeded, as a fine dose of smoke and heat is very difficult with large pieces of wood. In addition to the different types of wood, charcoal and briquettes are used, and sometimes combined. For example, since water smokers are heated solely with briquettes, the smoky flavor is achieved with wood chips or chunks that are soaked and placed into the flames. Chunks are rough pieces of wood that are larger than finely chopped chips and therefore smoke longer but with less smoke formation. Rotten or worm-eaten wood does not belong in a smoker, just as impregnated or even painted and varnished wood does not.

The selection of the type of wood is determined by what you would like to prepare in the smoker—and naturally according to the preferences of the pit boss.

This table of different wood types that are suitable for use in a smoker provides information as to the most common uses:

Food	Apple	Beech	Oak	Alder	Hickory	Cherry	Mesquite
Baking	≋	≋	≋	≋		≋	
Fish		≋	≋	≋			≋
Poultry	≋	≋	≋	≋	≋	≋	≋
Vegetables	≋	≋	≋	≋	≋		≋
Lamb		≋	≋	≋		≋	
Beef	≋	≋	≋	≋	≋	≋	≋
Pork	≋	≋	≋	≋	≋	≋	

Apple Wood

Well-dried apple wood gives barbecue dishes a lightly fruity, sweet taste. Apple trees are widespread and due to their high availability apple wood is often used. The energy value of most varieties is approximately 4 kW/kg.

Beech

Beech is an especially popular wood with high energy value, a fine smoky flavor, and an all-round wood for all smoker dishes.

Oak

Compared to beech wood, oak burns with somewhat higher temperatures at stronger smoke levels and like beech is universally usable and nearly neutral in taste.

Alder

With alder wood, a minor heat is produced with a fine, not all too powerful smoky flavor.

Hickory

This type of walnut tree is very prized in the States. If you use too much, the taste can easily become too intense. Nevertheless, the typical hickory flavor must be present at an authentic BBQ.

Cherry

Cherry wood gives the food a sweet, lightly fruity flavor and delights many a pit master.

Mesquite

From mesquite wood smoke jalapeño chili peppers you get an especially smoky hotness during smoking. Like chipotle, it is known as a chili specialty in the Tex-Mex kitchen. Mesquite wood is a classic from Texas, has a strong flavor, and is primarily used in wood chips or as a mix with softer types of wood.

Charcoal

Charcoal briquettes are frequently used as they often retain heat longer than pieces of wood. If they are of good quality, they can burn almost without odor for approximately three hours.

For kindling, a charcoal starter is the simplest and quickest solution. Here you place wax-saturated balls of wood shavings under the grate and fill the charcoal starter with briquettes. After approximately 20 minutes, when they have an almost white surface, they can be poured into the side firebox or the charcoal basket. Gloves should always be used for this.

Briquettes are well-suited as a fire base when combined with pieces of wood. The charcoal ensures the base heat, which can be adjusted higher with pieces of wood.

The charcoal starter

Wood Pellets

These small, standardized pellets can be burned in a special wood pellet grill instead of gas or charcoal and provide the heat in the smoker. The functionality of the pellets make wood pellet heating the more and more popular.

Wood pellets burn up to ninety-nine percent in the combustion chamber and thus a minimal amount of ash is left. The wood pellets are burned in a specially designed burner and provide a high energy value (approximately 5 kW/kg) with a small volume. The hot air from the burner and the smoke are led into a cooking chamber and provide the delicious smoky flavor of the food.

Only hardwood pellets should be used for grilling, barbecuing, baking, or smoking. These wood pellets contain 100 percent pure sawdust from the wood of deciduous trees, burn very efficiently, and, according to the variety, give the food a spicy smoky flavor.

The pellet expenditure, according to the device, is approximately 2 pounds [1 kilogram] per hour at low grilling temperatures 212° Fahrenheit–302° Fahrenheit (100 °C–150 °C) and approximately 5 1/2 pounds [2 1/2 kilograms] per hour at the highest temperature 518° Fahrenheit (270 °C).

Pellet hopper with electronic ignition and auger

3...2...1... Ignition !

To light the side firebox, small pieces of split wood are best suited as for example they can be placed in a diamond-shaped pattern on several pieces of beech wood. Wax-saturated balls of wood shavings are ideal to help start the fire. They burn five to ten minutes and produce a decent heat. The lid of the side firebox is always open in the process so the fire can work through from top to bottom. The reversed method, first kindling a small fire with split wood and then placing pieces of wood on top, is also practicable. However with the reversed method, more smoke is produced when lighting.

Using fluids to start a fire should be avoided, not only because of their partially toxic fumes, but also because simple wax-saturated balls of wood shavings work best and considerably reduce the risk of uncontrolled fire.

To bring the cooking chamber up to the right temperature you must close all lids after heating up and completely open the fan flap on the flue. The ventilation flap on the side firebox, from where the supply of oxygen is provided, is also opened. Thus, the flue draft starts and the smoker heats up. The temperature is first determined by the amount and type of wood used. The initial temperature, which quickly springs to over 392° Fahrenheit [200°C] according to the smoker, can be adjusted by opening the lid or closing the inlet again.

It is important that the smoker reaches a stable base heat and reliably maintains it. Only then can you start to put on the meat.

When the desired temperature of 194°–248° Fahrenheit [90°C–120°C] is reached, it is sufficient to add one piece of wood every 30 minutes for thick-walled smokers (wall thickness of .17" [4.5 mm] on). Well-constructed smokers store heat excellently and function with relatively little fuel over many hours. Naturally, the ambient temperature plays a role in winter as well as frequent opening of the lid. A rule of thumb is to keep the lid closed and open it only for mopping and adding on the meat. Pellet smokers are automatically relit every seven to ten minutes. The often thin metal of the cooking chamber makes this necessary.

With some practice, you will soon reach an even temperature with your smoker. Thermometers are used for monitoring. The thermometers built into a smoker often measure only the upper warm area of the cooking chamber. Here monitoring with an external thermometer is sensible.

Wood chips and chunks
for every taste

The BBQ market offers extensive accessories, and more are constantly being offered. In addition to quality and price, the personal preferences of the BBQ master are decisive when making a selection.

As when buying tools, whoever buys cheap often buys twice.

Here we present the most important BBQ utensils, of which you prefer to buy fewer, but look for good to very good quality. Experience has shown that too many accessories often spend their existence in the BBQ box, therefore, a precise purchasing budget with price comparisons is advisable.

ACCESSORIES

1. **Barbecue gloves:** They should have good insulation and be as long as possible. It is worth a visit to a specialized welding shop, not only because of the price.

2. **Silicone brush with a collection cup:** Here is a somewhat expensive model. It is sensible to gradually acquire several brushes in different widths and shapes.

3. **Brush:** The brush to clean the smoker grates should be as big as possible so that you can work on the large surfaces with corresponding pressure.

4. **Grate lifter:** A practical utensil with which you can lift hot grates.

5. **Spray bottle:** Necessary for spraying the food with non-viscous mixtures. Spraying is faster than mopping provided the mop sauce [the baste of barbecue] does not contain small pieces.

6. **Axe:** You should especially look for good quality to split pieces of wood with this tool.

7. **Turner:** This aid is available in every possible design and size for various fields of use. For fish, a large fish turner is beneficial.

8. **Digital probe thermometer:** With this tool the temperature of the meat can be quickly checked.

9. **Digital thermometer:** Available with and without radio stations. Modern thermometers are easy to operate, often have a built-in timer, and often have the various cooking temperatures saved. When reaching the set temperatures an audible signal sounds, and with it you are always on the safe side. So that the probe does not lie directly on the grate you can, for example, pierce a cork and stick the end of the probe inside. Thus you are able to measure the exact temperature over the grate.

10. **Mop with a bucket:** Large pieces of meat can be mopped with this.

11. **Grill tongs:** These are among the most important utensils for a BBQ, should fit well in your hands, and are easy to use. Before you buy them at the store it is best to see how they feel in your hands.

12. **Meat hook:** It is suited for turning and taking out heavier pieces of meat.

13. **Small grill brush with a scraper:** Minor fat crust can be removed from the grates with this.

14. **Thermally insulated silicone gloves:** They are suited excellently, for example, for pulling pulled pork.

*Wax-saturated balls of
wood shavings for clean and
quick fuel lighting.*

Wood planks are ideal for preparing tender meat and fish. They are soaked for at least three hours before they are placed on the grate. Preheated at high, direct heat, for example in the side fire box, the food is then placed on the planks in the smoker, and the planks give the food its fine flavor. With proper use and sufficient thickness they can often be used multiple times.

You can never have enough knives, but less is more here. The knives that you use daily should be of the best quality, easily sharpened, and be well balanced in your hands. Handling grinding stones has to be learned and is a rather painstaking task with Japanese knives because these normally cannot be resharpened with commercially available grinding instruments.

Part 2
THE DISHES

SPECIAL SEASONING

Meat, especially when it comes from the smoker or grill, tastes wonderful and unique. But it would quickly become boring if you did not have endless spices, herbs, and tricks on hand from which you can make something different from the same cut of meat time and again.

There are a countless number of rubs, spice blends, pastes, sauces, and marinades. Those that are presented here serve as a basis and can naturally be varied according to individual preferences. Thus, you will certainly, quickly find your own special favorite improvements for meat. That alone is a pleasure...

It doesn't matter if it's a rub, mop, sauce, or smoke—seasoning is immensely important for BBQ, possibly even the most important factor. The following recipes should help you to experiment with seasonings and to figure out where your individual preferences lie. We present you with the basics with which you cannot go wrong. At the same time they form the basis with which each BBQer will quickly experiment with their own creations.

Many of the recipes in this chapter appear in slightly modified forms in different places. In those cases, they are specially adjusted to the type of meat and harmonize with another element, like a rub, mop, paste, or sauce.

RUBS

Rubs are elementary seasonings that give the meat its special flavor. The advantage is their long preservability provided that they are stored airtight and in a dark place. You can experiment wonderfully here with the ingredients and in this way easily create your individual favorite mixtures. Combinations with mops and sauces are likewise a pleasure, just like a sweet rub that, for example, is well-suited as the basis for a spicy sauce. The result is sweet & spicy.

Before use, the rubs should be shaken well so that they are properly mixed. With a little bit of practice you will be able to produce a rub from several ingredients on hand—completely without a recipe.

After thoroughly coating with the rub and massaging it into the food, the meat should rest for a while so that the flavors can develop.

Basic Pork Rub

The classic pork rub is perfect for smoked pork and naturally also for pulled pork. Due to the low salt content it can be used as well for cured meat. The black pepper gives the rub a pleasant hotness that is somewhat milder than that of chili peppers.

Ingredients:	½	cup	paprika, sweet
	¼	cup	sugar
	3	tbsp.	black pepper
	2	tbsp.	salt
	2	tsp.	mustard powder
	2	tsp.	cayenne pepper
	1	tsp.	white pepper

Preparation: Combine all ingredients and massage half of the mixture into the meat 12–24 hours before smoking, the other half shortly before.

Beef Ribs Rub

The sweet and spicy flavors are optimally combined in this rub. You can individually adjust the hotness by using mild or medium chili powder. For an extra hot variation add an additional tablespoon of cayenne pepper into the mixture. Perfect for beef ribs, this rub also goes well with brisket or smoked haunch.

Ingredients:	¼	cup	paprika, sweet
	¼	cup	chili powder, mild or medium
	¼	cup	brown sugar
	¼	cup	black pepper, ground
	1	tbsp.	cayenne pepper
	1	tbsp.	garlic, granulated
	1	tbsp.	salt

Preparation: Thoroughly mix all ingredients and amply apply to both sides of the ribs. Massage in well, marinate, and smoke to taste.

Best Odds Brisket Rub

This rub is most frequently used in Texas for brisket. It is simple to mix and has everything necessary to smoke a classic Texas BBQ brisket. The combination of sweet and salty is well balanced, and the rub can naturally be refined with your favorite spices.

Ingredients:	½	cup	paprika, sweet
	½	cup	brown sugar
	3	tbsp.	garlic powder
	3	tbsp.	onion powder
	2	tbsp.	oregano

Preparation: Mix all ingredients well and rub the brisket thoroughly on all sides with the rub. The remainder can be stored airtight, in a dark place.

Best Odds Rib Rub

This rub is excellent for beginners—it is mild and does not over-season the meat. You can also adjust it to be saltier, sweeter, or hotter, according to taste.

Ingredients:	½	cup	paprika, sweet
	3	tbsp.	mustard powder
	3	tbsp.	onion powder
	3	tbsp.	garlic powder
	2	tbsp.	basil, dried
	1	tbsp.	black pepper, ground
	1	tbsp.	salt

Preparation: Mix all ingredients well and store airtight in a dark place. If you prefer a somewhat sweeter rub, you can also add two tablespoons of brown sugar.

BRITU – Best Ribs in the Universe

In 1996 Mike Scrutchfield won the title "Best Ribs in the Universe" at the American Royal BBQ Invitational Championships with this recipe. Since then the recipe has appeared in every recipe collection and is found with the abbreviation BRITU. You should carefully measure out this mixture, otherwise the meat will easily become too salty.

Ingredients:	¼	cup	sugar
	¼	cup	table salt
	⅛	cup	brown sugar
	4	tsp.	chili powder
	2	tsp.	cumin, ground
	1	tsp.	celery salt
	1	tsp.	cayenne pepper
	1	tsp.	black pepper, ground
	1	tsp.	garlic, granulated
	1	tsp.	onion powder

Preparation: Mix all ingredients and sprinkle all around; let sit until the surface is moist and then smoke according to taste. Around the end of cooking time the ribs are brushed with a sweet BBQ sauce.

Chipotle Dry Rub

This fresh and spicy rub tastes deliciously like chipotle. But the ingredients must absolutely be finely ground, best with a spice mill or a food chopper. Smoked chipotles or chipotle powder provide an additional kick here. The rub goes well with brisket, all kinds of pork, and even steak.

Ingredients:	2–3		dried chipotle peppers
	3	tbsp.	black pepper
	2	tbsp.	oregano, dried
	1	tbsp.	coriander, dried, no seeds
	1		bay leaf
	1	tsp.	cumin, ground
	1	tsp.	onion powder
	1	tsp.	orange peel, ground or dried

Preparation: Finely grind or chop all ingredients and store airtight, in a dark place until use.

Kansas City Rib Rub

In KC they know ribs, and here comes the BBQ rub for the legendary Kansas City style ribs. The recipe consists mainly of brown sugar and caters to a sweeter taste. Therefore, it is also not suitable for higher temperatures because the sugar would burn. Combined with a spicy BBQ sauce ribs, this rub provides a sweet-spicy experience.

Ingredients:	½	cup	brown sugar
	¼	cup	paprika, sweet
	1	tbsp.	black pepper
	1	tbsp.	salt
	1	tbsp.	chili powder
	1	tbsp.	garlic powder
	1	tbsp.	onion powder
	1	tbsp.	cayenne pepper

Preparation: Mix all ingredients and store airtight in a dark place.

Magic Dust

Magic dust is a universal rub that, like a normal rub, is rubbed in before smoking, but can also be used as seasoning on finished meals. If you would like it somewhat hotter and spicier, you can increase the amount of mustard powder and pepper to half a cup each.

Ingredients:	½	cup	paprika, sweet
	¼	cup	salt
	¼	cup	sugar
	2	tbsp.	mustard powder
	¼	cup	chili powder
	¼	cup	caraway seed, ground
	2	tbsp.	black pepper, ground
	¼	cup	garlic, granulated
	2	tbsp.	cayenne pepper

Preparation: Mix all ingredients and store in a tightly sealed container. You can fill a shaker with a portion of the rub and place it next to the salt and pepper on the table for additional seasoning.

Memphis Style Rib Rub

Traditional Memphis style ribs are served dry, or rather as dry rubs. However, that does not mean that the meat is dry. There is simply no BBQ sauce. What is special is that absolutely no sugar is added. This pure flavor without sweetness is prized above all in Memphis.

Ingredients:	2	tbsp.	paprika powder, sweet
	1	tbsp.	salt
	1	tbsp.	onion powder
	1	tbsp.	black pepper, ground
	2	tsp.	cayenne pepper

Preparation: Mix all ingredients and store in an airtight container. The rub is evenly massaged into the ribs. They are only placed into the smoker when the surface is moist.

Quarter Cup Brisket Rub

This is a harmonic, sweet rub for beef brisket; you only need one unit of measurement for its preparation because all ingredients are used in equal parts. You can also vary the hotness here with your choice of chili powder.

Ingredients:	¼	cup	brown sugar
	¼	cup	salt (coarse salt is best)
	¼	cup	paprika, sweet
	¼	cup	chili powder (mild or hot according to taste)
	¼	cup	black pepper, ground

Preparation: Mix all ingredients and thoroughly massage into the brisket. The remainder is best stored airtight and in a dark place.

RUBS

Traditional Carolina Pulled Pork Rub

This fantastic rub for traditional Carolina pulled pork originates from Chuck Ozburn, food photographer and enthusiastic BBQer. Wonderfully balanced between sweet and salty, it has a hot chili flavor.

Ingredients:	2	tbsp.	salt
	2	tbsp.	sugar
	2	tbsp.	brown sugar
	2	tbsp.	cumin, ground
	2	tbsp.	chili powder
	2	tbsp.	black pepper, ground
	1	tbsp.	cayenne pepper
	¼	cup	paprika, sweet

Preparation: In a small bowl mix all ingredients well. Store airtight in a dark place.

PASTES

Chili Paste

This paste combines the freshness of citrus fruits with the hotness of chili peppers. After mixing, you should let the paste rest so that the flavors can develop. You can vary the hotness with the type of chili peppers you use.

Ingredients:			
			lemon juice
	½	tsp.	lemon zest
			lime juice
	½	tsp.	lime zest
			orange juice
	½	tsp.	orange zest
	½		green chili, more according to taste (diced, with or without seeds)
	5		garlic cloves, finely minced
	3	tbsp.	chili powder, mild
	1	tbsp.	olive oil
	1	tbsp.	paprika powder, sweet
	1	tsp.	cumin, ground
	1	tsp.	salt
	½	tsp.	oregano, dried
	¼	tsp.	cinnamon, ground

Preparation: Half a teaspoon of zest from each citrus fruit gives this marinade its special flavor. You can adjust the consistency with the amount of juice.

Poultry Paste

In this poultry paste for all kinds of poultry, orange, clove, and nutmeg flavors dominate. Simply double the amount of listed ingredients for a turkey.

Ingredients:			
	2	tbsp.	fresh ginger, grated
	2	tbsp.	brown sugar
	2	tbsp.	orange zest
	1	tbsp.	black pepper, finely ground
	1	tbsp.	salt
	¼	tsp.	nutmeg, ground
	¼	tsp.	cloves, ground
			olive oil

Preparation: Mix all ingredients and add olive oil until the desired consistency is reached.

In contrast to spices, fresh ingredients are used in the pastes. They are spicy pastes that are easy to spread on the food but are not fluid like a sauce. The meat gets a special flavor from them. Note that the shelf life of pastes is very limited due to their fresh ingredients. It is possible to first mix together the dry ingredients and then add the fresh ingredients as required and shortly before use. Many pastes can be mixed with some water, boiled, and used as a mop sauce. If the paste is too coarse for this, you can puree it with a hand blender.

Garlic-Parsley Paste

Garlic lovers enjoy this paste. It is versatile and goes equally well with meat, fish, and poultry.

Ingredients:
½	cup	fresh parsley
½	cup	olive oil
6		garlic cloves, finely minced
1	tsp.	cayenne pepper
1		lemon, juice and zest

Preparation: Combine the parsley, garlic, cayenne pepper, lemon juice, and zest in a food processor. While the processor is running, slowly add the oil and form an emulsion. The paste can be stored up to one week in the refrigerator.

Herb Paste

Ideal paste for beef. It is suitable for grilling, braising, or smoking.

Ingredients:
1	tbsp.	garlic, minced
2	tbsp.	fresh basil, chopped
2	tbsp.	fresh oregano, chopped
2	tbsp.	fresh parsley, chopped
2	tbsp.	fresh rosemary, chopped
4	tbsp.	olive oil
1½	tbsp.	seasoning salt according to taste
1	tbsp.	black pepper, ground

Preparation: Mix all ingredients in a mixer or food processor until smooth. Distribute evenly over the surface of the meat and massage in well.

Horseradish Paste

This paste has a quite exceptional hotness. Freshly prepared, it is very hot, but becomes milder throughout the cooking process.

Ingredients:
¾	cup	fresh horseradish, grated
½	cup	garlic, finely minced
¼	cup	salt
¼	cup	black pepper, ground
½	cup	olive oil
2	tbsp.	cumin, ground
1	tbsp.	Dijon mustard
1	tbsp.	brown sugar

Preparation: Mix all ingredients well. You can store this paste up to one week in the refrigerator.

Parmesan Paste

Italian herbs dominate this mild paste.

Ingredients:
½	cup	parmesan, grated
¼	cup	olive oil
¼	cup	red wine vinegar
2	tbsp.	basil, dried
2	tbsp.	oregano, dried
1	tbsp.	black pepper, ground
4		garlic cloves, finely minced

Preparation: Mix all ingredients well. You can store this paste up to one week in the refrigerator. A suitable alternative is another strong hard cheese, such as pecorino.

Because the mops consist of many different ingredients that react differently to heat, it is noted in each individual mop recipe how often you should mop with the corresponding sauce.

MOPS AND MARINADES

Originally a cleaning mop was used for mopping to protect large amounts of meat from drying out. The mop was dipped into the mop sauce and each piece of meat was also easily reached with it on a giant fireplace thanks to the long handle. Thus, the BBQ mop received its name.

Only a miniature version of the original mop is used in households today. They are mostly thick brushes made of silicon. However, the mop recipes have remained the same.

Best Odds Brisket Mop

This mop keeps the meat tender and savory while it is in the smoker. It is ideal for beef brisket.

Ingredients:	½	cup	apple cider vinegar
	¼	cup	olive oil
	¼	cup	beer
	3	tbsp.	paprika powder, sweet
	1	tsp.	salt
	1	tsp.	black pepper, ground

Preparation: Mix all ingredients until the salt has dissolved and mop the meat every two hours.

Beer Mop

The flavors of the spices together with the beer result in a very special taste.

Ingredients:	1½	cup	beer
	½	cup	apple cider vinegar
	½	cup	water
	½	cup	oil
	1		small onion, diced
	3		garlic cloves, finely minced
	1	tbsp.	Worcestershire sauce
	1	tsp.	black pepper, ground
	1	tsp.	salt
	1	tsp.	cayenne pepper

Preparation: Put everything into a pot, heat, and simmer until the garlic and onions are very soft. Regularly mop the meat every two hours.

Bourbon Mop

This sweet mop sauce is refined with bourbon. It goes wonderfully with beef and pork.

Ingredients:	1	cup	Kentucky bourbon
	½	cup	brown sugar
	½	cup	onions, very finely diced, nearly pureed
	¼	cup	sugar beet syrup
	¼	cup	ketchup
	2	tbsp.	Dijon mustard

Preparation: Mix all ingredients well. You can store the mop in the refrigerator and should not use it when it is too hot because the sugar can quickly burn. Thoroughly mop the meat every two hours with the sauce.

Carolina Lemon Mop

This vinegar-based mop has an excellent lemon flavor that goes remarkably well with pork from the smoker. You can adjust the hotness with the addition of Tabasco sauce according to taste.

Ingredients:	1	cup	apple cider vinegar
	½	cup	water
	3	tbsp.	lemon juice
	2	tbsp.	butter, melted
	2	tbsp.	Worcestershire sauce
	2	tbsp.	sugar
	2	tsp.	Tabasco sauce
	1	tsp.	cayenne pepper

Preparation: Mix all ingredients and it is best to let sit overnight so that the flavors can completely develop. Mop the meat once per hour with the sauce.

Carolina Style Pulled Pork Mop

This mop goes wonderfully with the traditional Carolina pulled pork. You can use it as both a normal mop sauce and as sauce for pulled pork.

Ingredients:	1	cup	apple cider vinegar
	2	tbsp.	salt
	1	tbsp.	brown sugar
	1	tsp.	cayenne pepper
	1	tsp.	chili flakes

Preparation: Mix all ingredients until the sugar dissolves. If you would like to use the sauce for the finished meat you can also add some ketchup or BBQ sauce. Mop the meat every two hours with the sauce.

One-For-All Mop

This mop can be used universally, as it goes well with pork, beef, poultry, and lamb.

Ingredients:	2	cups	apple cider vinegar
	2	cups	water
	1	tsp.	garlic powder
	2	tsp.	poultry seasoning
	6		bay leaves
	1	tsp.	red pepper, ground
	1	tsp.	thyme, dried
	1	tsp.	rosemary, dried
	1	tsp.	lemon pepper
	1	tsp.	salt
	1	tsp.	black pepper, ground

Preparation: Bring all ingredients to a boil and simmer for 30 minutes. The mop should cool down before use. Mop the meat every 2 hours with the sauce.

Lamb Mop

This mop is the actual secret of the classic Kentucky mutton barbecue. The combination of beer and oil together with the spices gives the smoked lamb its typical flavor.

Ingredients:	1	cup	apple cider vinegar
	1	cup	water
	1	cup	beer (or beef broth)
	¼	cup	Worcester sauce
	2	tbsp.	black pepper, ground
	1	tbsp.	brown sugar
	½	tbsp.	salt
	½	tbsp.	garlic powder
	1	tsp.	cayenne pepper

Preparation: Heat all ingredients in a pot over low heat and mop the lamb once per hour.

Turkey and Poultry Mop

This mop is suited for whole poultry. It does not matter if it's smoked or grilled, it keeps the meat juicy and helps to brown the skin.

Ingredients:

½	cup	butter
1	tbsp.	lemon juice
1	tsp.	poultry seasoning
1	tsp.	basil, dried
1	tsp.	thyme, dried
1	tsp.	sage, dried

Preparation: Melt the butter in a pot and add the lemon juice and spices. After the first hour mop the poultry every 30 minutes.

Rib Mop

This mop is suitable for all types of pork ribs. The vinegar gives the meat its tenderness, the herbs its flavor. It naturally goes well with other pork dishes.

Ingredients:

½	cup	water
½	cup	vinegar
3	tbsp.	mustard
3	tbsp.	olive oil
1	tbsp.	chili powder
1	tbsp.	garlic powder
1	tsp.	cayenne pepper

Preparation: Mix all ingredients well and store in the refrigerator. If stored cold, you can preserve the mop for approximately three months. Mop the ribs once per hour with the sauce.

MOPS AND MARINADES

Texas Hillbilly Mop

What is special about this mop is that there is no sugar. It will not burn and is suitable for all types of beef.

Ingredients:

2	cups	vinegar
1	cup	olive oil
½	cup	Worcester sauce
½	cup	water
2		lemons, pressed and quartered
2	tbsp.	hot chili sauce
6		bay leaves, ground
2		garlic cloves, finely minced
1	tbsp.	paprika powder, sweet
1	tbsp.	chili powder

Preparation: Put all ingredients into a pot, mix, and bring to a boil. Remove from heat, but keep warm. Mop the meat once per hour.

BARBECUE SAUCES

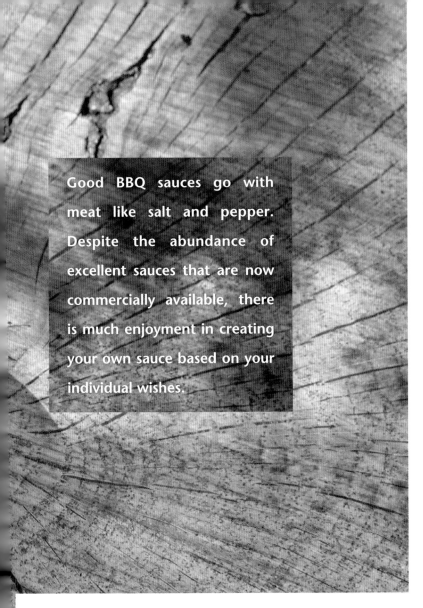

Good BBQ sauces go with meat like salt and pepper. Despite the abundance of excellent sauces that are now commercially available, there is much enjoyment in creating your own sauce based on your individual wishes.

Classic BBQ Rib Sauce

If you prefer thick and substantial sauces for your ribs, you will like this sauce. Tomato puree and tomato paste replace ketchup here from which the sauce gets a mild and harmonic tartness.

Ingredients:	2	cups	tomato puree
	1	cup	tomato paste
	¼	cup	onions, finely diced
	2	tbsp.	brown sugar
	2	tbsp.	vinegar
	2	tbsp.	olive oil
	3		garlic cloves, crushed
	1	tbsp.	Worcestershire sauce
	1	tsp.	mustard powder
	1	tsp.	cayenne pepper
			black pepper, freshly ground according to taste

Preparation: Cook the diced onions with the garlic in olive oil until transparent. Add the other ingredients and simmer everything for 20 minutes. Let cool before serving.

Best Odds Pulled Pork Sauce

This sauce is added to the meat after pulling (see page 65). It is best to mix the warm sauce with the warm meat.

Ingredients:	1½	cups	apple cider vinegar
	½	cup	hot water
	2	tbsp.	brown sugar
	1	tbsp.	paprika powder, sweet
	1	tsp.	black pepper, ground
	1	tsp.	salt
	1	tsp.	cayenne pepper

Preparation: Dissolve the sugar in the water and then add the remaining ingredients. Make sure that when mixing with the meat that the mixture becomes neither too dry nor too soupy.

Chicken Sauce

While the pulled pork or brisket is being smoked, you need something as a snack in the meantime. We recommend a chicken sandwich with this sauce.

Ingredients:	2	cups	apple cider vinegar
	4	tbsp.	tomato paste
	1½	tbsp.	sugar
	1½	tbsp.	peanut oil
	1½	tbsp.	salt
	1	tbsp.	steak sauce
	1	tbsp.	Worcestershire sauce
	½	tbsp.	hot chili sauce

Preparation: Let all ingredients simmer in a pot for ten minutes. One half is used to marinate the chicken before barbecuing, the other half is brushed on during barbecuing.

Alabama White Barbecue Sauce

In Alabama, mayonnaise is traditionally used as the sauce base instead of tomato sauce. This sauce may only be applied at the very end of cooking time because it would otherwise separate. It goes well with poultry and pork and has a spicy, harmonic taste.

Ingredients:	2	cups	mayonnaise
	1	cup	apple cider vinegar
	2	tbsp.	lemon juice
	3	tbsp.	black pepper, ground
	1	tsp.	salt
	½	tsp.	cayenne pepper

Preparation: Mix all ingredients cold and let marinate 4–5 hours in the refrigerator. The sauce also works well as a dip, so always save a little.

Jack Daniel's Rib Glaze

This sauce may also only be used at the end of the cooking time. It should certainly become hot but not burn.

Ingredients:	1	cup	Jack Daniel's whisky
	1	cup	ketchup
	½	cup	brown sugar
	¼	cup	vinegar
	1	tbsp.	lemon juice
	2	tsp.	Worcestershire sauce
	3		garlic cloves, finely minced
	1	tsp.	mustard powder
			salt and pepper according to taste

Preparation: Heat all ingredients in a pot and simmer for 20 minutes. If you make this sauce a few days in advance, the flavors can better develop.

Mustard Barbecue Sauce

If you are not familiar with a barbecue sauce with a mustard base, you should try this one. It goes well with almost everything, but it is best with pork.

Ingredients:	1	cup	medium mustard
	½	cup	balsamic vinegar
	¼	cup	brown sugar
	2	tbsp.	butter
	1	tbsp.	Worcestershire sauce
	1	tbsp.	lemon juice
	1	tsp.	cayenne pepper

Preparation: Mix all ingredients and cook over low heat for 30 minutes. The hotter the mustard, the hotter the sauce, so here you can modify according to taste.

Piedmont Barbecue Sauce

This classic sauce from the "birthplace" of BBQ, the Piedmont, is relatively runny and yet full of flavor.

Ingredients:	1½	cups	apple cider vinegar
	½	cup	ketchup
	½	cup	water
	1	tbsp.	sugar
	1	tsp.	salt
	¼	tsp.	chili powder

Preparation: Mix all ingredients and store airtight in a dark place.

Chickasha Hot Sauce

Originally, the main ingredient in this sauce, which was invented in the '80s, was a "finished" BBQ sauce. Much has changed and improved, and today everything possible is in it except for one thing: an *ultimate, final* BBQ sauce recipe.

Ingredients:	3	cups	ketchup
	1	cup	sugar beet syrup
	½	cup	red wine vinegar
	3	tbsp.	Worcester sauce
	2	tsp.	Tabasco sauce
	½	cup	lime juice
	½		onion, finely diced
	2		garlic cloves, finely minced
	½	cup	brown sugar
	3	tsp.	mustard powder
	1	tsp.	cayenne pepper
	2	cups	water

Preparation: Mix all the ingredients, except for the water, in a pot. Add water until a cream-like consistency develops. Bring to a boil and simmer for one hour. If the sauce becomes too thick, add some water again.

Hot Vinegar Sauce

This sauce gives the meat a special kick. It goes well with pulled pork, but you must be careful with the vinegar, it is better to use too little than too much.

Ingredients:	1	cup	water
	1	tbsp.	salt
	¼	cup	apple cider vinegar
	3	tbsp.	Tabasco sauce
	1	tbsp.	black pepper, freshly ground
	1	tbsp.	oregano, dried
	¼	cup	brown sugar
	1	tbsp.	paprika powder
	1	tbsp.	garlic powder

Preparation: Mix all ingredients, bring to a boil, and serve warm.

Amarillo Sauce

Typical Texas beef already appears here in the sauce—at least sensorially. It is prepared with a beef broth and goes well with brisket or steak for the in-between times.

Ingredients:	2	cups	ketchup
	2	cups	water
	2	tsp.	instant beef broth
	1	tsp.	mustard powder
	1	tbsp.	chili powder
	1	tsp.	black pepper, freshly ground
	½	tsp.	cayenne
	½	tsp.	garlic powder
	½	tsp.	smoked salt
	2	tsp.	Worcester sauce
	3	tbsp.	brown sugar
	1	tsp.	lime juice

Preparation: Mix all ingredients and bring to a boil. Then simmer for 15 minutes while stirring. Let cool and serve.

PORK

In the South, when people talk about BBQ, they mean pork. Individual preferences are very different: many palates prefer the shoulder, others favor the ribs. Even if everything once began as a "whole hog BBQ" you can also optimally prepare cuts with the mobile smokers available today.

Pork shoulder or neck are filled with fat and thus provide a juicy experience. If you cook a roast pork with crackling at a higher temperature, you're delighted by the crispy, delicious crust. Ribs provide variety with the number of possibilities for preparation while classics like pulled pork demand the dedication of the pit master for hours.

It does not matter which cut you choose: in comparison to other types of meat, pork is in the lower and mid-range price. An advantage of using pork is that there are no big impacts if your measurements are slightly off on the chili powder in the rub.

PULLED PORK

When preparing pulled pork (PP) the pork is cooked at a low temperature (see box) until it falls apart or until you can pull it without any tools. This step applies to all PP recipies.

Rubs and mops, which can be combined with each other as desired, provide the individual flavor.

A few TIPS for perfect pulled pork:

≈ The temperature should never exceed 230° Fahrenheit [110°C]. The meat would then cook faster but would not be as tender and juicy.

≈ Allow for sufficient time. With 20 hours you are always on the safe side. The finished, cooked meat is best stored wrapped in aluminum foil in a cooler before pulling. It becomes even more tender and juicier in the process. So preferably finish earlier instead of waiting.

≈ At approximately 160°–170° Fahrenheit [72°C–77°C] the so-called plateau phase starts when the tendons and connective tissues break down. Energy is needed for this, dropping the core temperature. Don't let yourself get worked up over this, and do not raise the pit temperature.

≈ Opening and closing the lid is poison for BBQ. The lid should only be opened for mopping.

≈ Shoulders or necks are ideal for PP; both are very marbled and have intense flavor.

≈ PP is perfectly suited for freezing and heating. Do not be put off by the quantity, but rather also think about tomorrow—if anything is left over...

Pulling Step-by-Step

After 16–20 hours of cooking time in the smoker the core temperature is 203° Fahrenheit [95°C] and the meat is ready to be pulled. Thermally insulated gloves protect your hands from the hot meat.

Only with your hands, no other aids, pull apart the meat. In the photograph you see the topside without bones. With a shoulder, the shoulder blade is pulled from the meat without anything hanging on it.

The inner, light, tender meat is thoroughly mixed with the crispy, smoky-spicy crust. This way the different textures and flavors are mixed well with each other.

An important component of pulled pork is a good sauce, which is now added. It intensifies the flavor and provides the necessary juiciness. If the meat is still too mild, you can add seasoning at this point.

Together with the sauce everything is thoroughly mixed once more, and in the process, larger pieces are broken up into small pieces.

You can serve pulled pork with coleslaw on a burger bun (see below)—for many smoker fans the only true way to enjoy PP.

Jamaican Jerk

In Jamaica there are pigs, and people who are also familiar with BBQ. Only the name is different. There it is called *jerk*. A classic jerk recipe from this Caribbean island is prepared as follows:

Ingredients: Jerk rub

6	tbsp.	onion powder
6	tbsp.	fried onions
2	tbsp.	allspice, ground
2	tbsp.	black pepper, freshly ground
2	tbsp.	cayenne pepper
2	tbsp.	sugar
4½	tsp.	thyme, dried
1½	tsp.	nutmeg, ground
½	tsp.	chili powder

Meat

| 6–11 lbs. | | pork shoulder, without rind, or a corresponding piece of neck |

Jerk mop

The other half of the jerk rub
that is not needed for rubbing

| 3 | cups | apple cider vinegar |
| 1 | | onion, cut into small strips |

Preparation:
1. The day before barbecuing, mix the rub ingredients and massage the meat well with half of the rub. Wrap the meat tightly in foil and let marinate overnight in the refrigerator.
2. Take the meat out of the refrigerator four hours before barbecuing and let sit at room temperature.
3. Heat the smoker to approximately 212° Fahrenheit [100°C].
4. Mix the mop ingredients and heat over a low flame until the rub has dissolved in the vinegar.
5. Place the meat into the smoker and cook until a core temperature of 194°–203° Fahrenheit [90°C–95°C] is reached. While cooking, the meat is thoroughly mopped every 1½ hours.
6. Wrap the finished meat in aluminum foil and let sit for 20 minutes, then pull and mix with a good sauce. Here a fruity-hot sauce or a chutney works well.

Memphis Style Pulled Pork

The favorite PP of Elvis, the King of Rock 'n' Roll, is both sweet and hot. It is not mopped, but its own sauce is added.

Ingredients: Memphis rub

2	tbsp.	paprika powder, sweet
1	tbsp.	salt
1	tbsp.	onion powder
2	tbsp.	black pepper, freshly ground
1½	tsp.	cayenne pepper

Meat

| 3 | kg. | whole pork neck |

Memphis BBQ sauce

2	cups	ketchup
2	cups	onions, diced
1	cup	red wine vinegar
2		garlic cloves, minced
¼	cup	mustard
¼	cup	brown sugar
1	tsp.	Tabasco sauce

Preparation:
1. The day before barbecuing, mix the rub ingredients and massage the meat well with half of the rub. Tightly wrap the meat in foil and let marinate overnight in the refrigerator.
2. Take the meat out of the refrigerator four hours before barbecuing, let sit at room temperature, and massage with the second half of the rub.
3. Heat the smoker to approximately 212° Fahrenheit [100°C], place the meat into the smoker, and cook until a core temperature of 194°–203° Fahrenheit [90°C–95°C] is reached.
4. In the meantime mix the ingredients for the sauce in a pot, simmer until the onions are soft, and let cool.
5. After cooking is done, wrap the meat in aluminum foil, let sit for 20 minutes, then pull and mix with half of the sauce. Serve with coleslaw and the remaining BBQ sauce on a burger bun.

Tex-Mex Pulled Pork

This recipe comes from Texas. The meat does without a rub and mop and instead is rubbed initially with a sauce. Then you do not have to do anything more...

Ingredients:	Sauce		
	2	cups	tomato puree
	3–4		green chilies, diced
	1	cup	BBQ sauce according to taste
	½		onion, diced
	½	cup	coriander, chopped
	4	tbsp.	chili powder
	1	tsp.	oregano, dried
	1	tsp.	cumin, ground
	½	tsp.	cinnamon
	½	tsp.	black pepper, freshly ground

	Meat		
	6½	lbs.	pork loin, without bones

Preparation:
1. Take the meat out of the refrigerator four hours before barbecuing and let sit at room temperature.
2. Heat the smoker to approximately 212° Fahrenheit [100°C].
3. Mix the ingredients for the sauce, except for the coriander, and heat over a low flame until everything has dissolved and the onions are soft.
4. Thoroughly rub the meat with the sauce, place into the smoker, and cook until a core temperature of 194°–203° Fahrenheit [90°C–95°C] is reached.
5. Now wrap in aluminum foil and let sit for 20 minutes. Then pull and mix with the remaining sauce and coriander.

If you prepare pork in the smoker at temperatures around 212° Fahrenheit [100°C], you must remove the rind. It becomes leathery and tough, furthermore it prevents the rub and mop from penetrating the meat and takes up valuable crust surface.

The Renowned Mr. Brown

In southern slang "Mr. Brown" refers to the dark and smoky outside of smoked pork. The constant evolution of this old recipe has made it what the name already suggests: *famous*.

Ingredients:	Southern succor rub		
	¼	cup	black pepper, freshly ground
	¼	cup	paprika powder, sweet
	¼	cup	brown sugar
	2	tbsp.	salt
	2	tbsp.	mustard powder
	1	tsp.	cayenne pepper

	Meat		
	3–5	kg.	pork shoulder, without rind, or a corresponding piece of neck

Southern mop
The other half of the southern succor rub that is not required for rubbing.

	2	cups	apple cider vinegar
	1	cup	water
	3	tbsp.	black pepper, freshly ground
	2	tbsp.	salt
	1	tbsp.	Worcester sauce
	1	tbsp.	paprika powder, sweet
	1	tbsp.	cayenne pepper

Preparation:
1. The day before barbecuing mix the rub ingredients and massage the meat with half of the rub. Wrap the meat tightly in foil and let marinate overnight in the refrigerator.
2. Take the meat out of the refrigerator four hours before barbecuing and let sit at room temperature.
3. Heat the smoker to approximately 212° Fahrenheit [100°C].
4. Mix the mop ingredients and heat over a low flame until everything has dissolved.
5. Place the meat into the smoker and cook until a core temperature of 194°–203° Fahrenheit [90°C–95°C] is reached. Thoroughly mop every 1½ hours.
6. Wrap the cooked meat in aluminum foil and let sit for 20 minutes, then pull and mix with a BBQ sauce according to taste.

RIBS

Among the classic BBQ dishes, there are numerous variations for ribs. They are already edible after ten minutes on the grill ... but this has nothing to do with BBQ ribs, which have earned this name. "Real" BBQ ribs have a different cut, and they differ in seasoning. If they are brushed with a sauce and smoked, they're called wet ribs. If they remain dry for the entire cooking time, they are called dry ribs. There are also many different methods of preparation that all have one thing in common: good ribs need a lot of time and low temperatures. Otherwise they become hard and tough, and they do not come loose from the bone. If you like that chewy texture, you can naturally prepare ribs, at high cooking temperatures, which you can nibble on, but the goal here is to reach the "fall off the bone" stage. And you are most successful when you stick to the following points:

Open, low, & slow:

The ribs are thoroughly rubbed and then placed in the smoker with the flesh side up. Here they are slowly cooked at 230° Fahrenheit [110°C] for 4–6 hours until the meat pulls back and the ends of the bones are showing. If the bones can be pulled from the meat, the slabs are either brushed with a BBQ sauce and cooked slightly longer (wet ribs) or are taken from the smoker (dry ribs). Smoke is also used as desired.

Precooking:

The rubbed slabs are packed as airtight as possible. Aluminum foil can be used or, for larger amounts, a heat-resistant baking dish that also is tightly sealed with aluminum foil. Packed in this way, the slabs are precooked either with or without sauce for 2 $^1/_2$–3 hours at 230° Fahrenheit [110°C]. This can be done in a smoker or an oven because the meat cannot absorb smoke through the foil anyway. They are virtually steamed in their own juice and during this process become extremely tender and soft. Then they are unpacked, carefully placed in the smoker, and brushed with a BBQ sauce. After approximately 1 $^1/_2$ hours and being glazed 2–3 times, the ribs are finished. With this method the smoky flavor is very subtle. This is because the meat usually absorbs the smoke most intensively at the beginning, i.e. when these ribs are still packed airtight.

3-2-1:

A very popular method is the 3–2–1 method. It is a combination of the first two versions. After applying the rub, first smoke for three hours as normal, then wrapped for two hours, and then again one hour open for glazing.

Precooking:

For this version the ribs are precooked in salt water. They certainly become tender but taste cured, like Kassler. Among insiders this method is considered unsportsmanlike and is almost never practiced.

Preparing Ribs

The various cuts are an additional distinguishing feature of ribs. First the complete rib side is roughly cut into two pieces. The top portion has approximately 4″ [10 cm] long bones and is meaty. These are the first 4″ [10 cm] that are directly attached to the spine. In the language of BBQ they are called "loin" or "baby back" ribs. Underneath are the spare ribs. They are longer than the baby back ribs and end in the breast cartilage. If you cut this off a trim is created that is called the St. Louis cut, another very famous cut.

On the bone side there is a thin, silver membrane. This periosteum must be removed because it prevents the spices of

the rubs or marinades from sinking into the meat. Additionally, it is very difficult to chew. To best remove this membrane, use a blunt object, such as a screwdriver, and a paper towel. Slide the screwdriver between the bone and membrane and pull it with the paper towel. Sometimes this is achieved in one piece.

Before the ribs are rubbed and you begin with the BBQ some work is necessary. Here you can see how a genuine St. Louis cut is made from a simple rib side.

1 The entire rib side. The belly can be seen in the front. The baby backs are on the other side.

2 With a sharp knife the breast cartilage at the base of the bone is cut.

3 The white cartilage ends are called "rib tips."

4 Now the membrane must be removed. Using a paper towel as an aid...

5 ...it is usually successful in one pull.

6 Loose pieces of meat and cartilage remnants are simply cut off.

7 Now just the rub is missing, and then you're ready to go.

Apple City Baby Backs

This recipe with apple flavor comes from the BBQers from Murphysboro, Illinois.

Ingredients:

Cheryl's Cider Soak

1½	cups	apple juice or cider
½	cup	apple cider vinegar
½		onion, diced
1½	tbsp.	Worcester sauce
1	tbsp.	olive oil
1	tsp.	cinnamon
1	tsp.	thyme, dried

Meat

2	slabs	baby back ribs

Apple Rib Rub

¼	cup	brown sugar
4	tsp.	onion powder
1	tsp.	cinnamon
1	tsp.	mustard powder
1	tsp.	salt
½	tsp.	thyme, dried

Apple Rib Mop

1½	cups	apple juice or cider
½	cup	apple cider vinegar
4	tsp.	Worcester sauce

Apple City Apple Sauce

½	cup	butter
1		onion, finely diced
2½	cups	apple juice or cider
2	tbsp.	sugar beet syrup
2	tbsp.	Worcester sauce
2	tbsp.	apple cider vinegar
2	tbsp.	tomato paste
½	tsp.	chili powder
½	tsp.	cinnamon
½	tsp.	salt

Preparation:

1. The day before barbecuing, combine the soak ingredients, add the ribs, and marinate in the refrigerator.
2. Mix the rub ingredients well and set aside.
3. Take the ribs out three hours before barbecuing, dry, and rub with approximately half of the rub. Massage in the second half shortly before smoking.
4. Heat the smoker to 230° Fahrenheit [110°C], and smoke the ribs for four hours.
5. In the meantime, mix the mop sauce, warm slightly, and mop the ribs once per hour.
6. In the last hour, glaze with the apple sauce two times. The ribs are done when they almost fall from the bone and the sauce caramelizes.

Bourbon-Glazed Ribs

Eating whisky in a sauce on ribs is just as much fun as drinking it. The sauce is not confined to the ribs—you should definitely place some in a bowl on the table.

Ingredients:

Rib Rub

½	cup	pepper, freshly ground
¼	cup	paprika powder, sweet
2	tbsp.	sugar
1	tbsp.	coarse salt
1	tbsp.	chili powder
1½	tsp.	garlic powder
1½	tsp.	onion powder

Meat

3	slabs	St. Louis cut (or 4 slabs baby back ribs)

Bourbon Mop

½	cup	bourbon
½	cup	apple cider vinegar

Bour Whisky BBQ Sauce

¼	cup	butter
¼	cup	olive oil
2		onions, finely diced
¾	cup	bourbon
½	cup	ketchup
½	cup	apple cider vinegar
½	cup	orange juice
½	cup	maple syrup
2	tbsp.	Worcester sauce
½	tsp.	black pepper, freshly ground
½	tsp.	salt

Preparation:

1. The day before barbecuing, combine the rub ingredients, spread half on the ribs, and massage in well. Wrap the ribs in foil and keep cold.
2. Unwrap the ribs three hours before barbecuing and rub with the second half of the rub.
3. Heat the smoker to 230° Fahrenheit [110°C] and smoke the ribs as normal for four hours.
4. In the meantime mix the mop sauce, warm slightly, and mop the ribs after 1 1/2 and 3 hours.
5. Meanwhile heat the butter and oil for the sauce and lightly sauté the onions in it for five minutes. Add the remaining ingredients and let everything simmer together for 40 minutes.
6. Thoroughly brush the ribs with the sauce 45 minutes before the end of the cooking time and possibly repeat this step once more.
7. Boil down the remainder of the sauce to approximately one third and serve with the ribs.
8. The ribs are done when the meat is tender, the sauce is thick and "sticky," and the surface shines. Serve with additional BBQ sauce according to taste.

Fruity Style Cinnamon Ribs

These are the champions of the ribs category at a German barbecue championship. Masterful.

Ingredients: Rub

2	tsp.	garlic, granulated
3	tbsp.	salt
10	tbsp.	natural brown sugar
2	tsp.	celery salt
2	tsp.	chili flakes
2	tsp.	thyme, dried
2	tsp.	pepper

Meat

4	slabs	baby back ribs

Sauce

4	cups	orange juice
8	tbsp.	Worcester sauce
8	tbsp.	balsamic vinegar
12		garlic cloves, pureed
1	inch	ginger, peeled and grated
12	tbsp.	sugar beet syrup
4	tsp.	cinnamon
12	tbsp.	honey
8	tbsp.	Tabasco sauce

Preparation:
1. The day before barbecuing, combine the rub ingredients, spread on the ribs, and massage in well. Wrap the ribs in foil and keep cold over night.
2. Mix all ingredients for the sauce and heat until the sugar beet syrup and honey have dissolved.
3. With the meaty side up, place the ribs on aluminum foil sheets, approximately 12" x 16" [30 cm x 40 cm], and pull the edges slightly upward. Spread the heated sauce onto this little package and close the aluminum foil as airtight as possible.
4. Bring the smoker to 230° Fahrenheit [110°C] and cook the pack for 2–2 ½ hours.
5. Carefully unwrap the slabs. They are now very tender. Collect the sauce in a bowl, strain, and reduce to one third.
6. Then finish the ribs as normal for one hour at 248° Fahrenheit [120°C] in the smoker; in the process glaze two to three times with the sauce.

Kansas City Sloppy Finger-Lickin' Ribs

This recipe comes from Kansas City. You should certainly make sure that enough napkins are available because—as the name suggests—it is very messy...

Ingredients: Finger-Lickin' Rub

1	cup	brown sugar
½	cup	paprika powder, sweet
2½	tbsp.	black pepper, freshly ground
2½	tbsp.	coarse salt
1½	tbsp.	chili powder
1½	tbsp.	onion powder
1–2	tsp.	cayenne pepper

Meat

3	slabs	St. Louis cut or 4 slabs of baby back ribs

Kansas City Masterpiece BBQ Sauce
(from specialist retailer)

Preparation:
1. The day before barbecuing, combine the rub ingredients, spread one third on the ribs, and massage in well. Then wrap the ribs in foil and keep cold.
2. Unwrap the ribs three hours before barbecuing and rub with another third of the rub.
3. Heat the smoker to 230° Fahrenheit [110°C] and smoke the ribs as normal for four hours. Sprinkle the last third of the rub on after half of the time has elapsed.
4. Thoroughly brush the ribs with the sauce 45 minutes before the end of the cooking time and possibly repeat this process once more.
5. The ribs are done when the meat is tender and the sauce is thick and "sticky."
6. Serve with additional BBQ sauce.

Lone Star Ribs

In contrast to the wet ribs with BBQ sauce that are prepared on the East Coast, these ribs that are typical for Texas remain dry.

Ingredients: Lone Star Rub

½	cup	pepper, freshly ground
¼	cup	paprika powder
2	tbsp.	sugar
1	tbsp.	salt
1	tbsp.	chili powder
1½	tsp.	garlic powder
1½	tsp.	onion powder

Meat

3	slabs	St. Louis cut or 4 slabs of baby back ribs

Lone Star Mop

½	cup	water
2	cups	beer
½	cup	apple cider vinegar
¼	cup	olive oil
½		onion, diced
2	bulbs	garlic, finely minced
1	tbsp.	Worcester sauce
1	tbsp.	Lone Star rub

Preparation:

1. The day before barbecuing, combine the rub ingredients, spread half on the ribs, massage in well, wrap the ribs in foil, and keep cold.
2. Unwrap the ribs three hours before barbecuing and rub with the second half of the rub. Set aside one tablespoon of the rub.
3. Heat the smoker to 230° Fahrenheit [110°C] and smoke the ribs for 5–6 hours.
4. In the meantime, mix the mop sauce, warm slightly, and mop the ribs once per hour. They are done when they nearly fall off of the bones.

Thai Phoon Baby Backs

Asiatic flavors go magnificently with ribs, so why not try Thai style once? With the matching dip, these ribs are wonderfully suited as finger food.

Ingredients: Thai Phoon Marinade

1½	cups	pineapple pieces
2	tbsp.	fish sauce, alternatively soy sauce
¼	cup	lime juice
3		garlic cloves, finely minced
1½	blades	lemon grass, chopped

Meat

2	slabs	baby back ribs

Thai Phoon Dipping Mop

2	tbsp.	peanut oil
½	blade	lemon grass, chopped
2		garlic cloves, finely minced
1½	cups	pineapple pieces
¾	cup	apple cider vinegar
¼	cup	sugar
2	tbsp.	fish sauce
1–2	tsp.	chili flakes
1–2	tbsp.	coriander, chopped

Preparation:

1. The day before barbecuing, finely puree the ingredients for the marinade and place the slabs in it. Turn occasionally so that the marinade can sink in all over.
2. Take the ribs out three hours before barbecuing, drain, and bring the marinade with a $^1/_2$ cup water to a boil. The boiled marinade serves as a mop sauce for the ribs.
3. Heat the smoker to 230° Fahrenheit [110°C] and smoke the ribs for four hours.
4. In the meantime mix the mop sauce, warm slightly, and mop the ribs with it once per hour.
5. Cook the lemon grass and the garlic for the dip for five minutes in oil over a low flame until soft. Add the remaining ingredients except for the coriander, boil, and reduce to one third. Finally stir in the coriander and serve the dip warm with the ribs.

SPECIALS

Aside from the classics, pulled pork and ribs, there is naturally a number of alternative pork dishes that are excellently suited for preparation in the smoker. The selection of smokers to use, which you can heat to different temperatures, is vast.

Stuffed Pork Loin Mexicano

The combination of a fruit salsa with spicy chorizo gives this dish real pep. It is certainly elaborate but worth the effort.

Ingredients:

Sweet Sensation Rub

1	tbsp.	allspice, ground
1	tbsp.	brown sugar
1	tbsp.	onion powder
1½	tsp.	salt
½	tsp.	nutmeg, ground
½	tsp.	cinnamon
½	tsp.	thyme, dried

Meat

Approx.	9 lbs.	pork loin, lengthwise with a pocket for the stuffing

Salsa

1	cup	orange juice
2		ripe tomatoes
1		ripe banana, diced
½		onion, finely diced
1		fresh chili pepper, finely diced
2	tsp.	olive oil
1	tsp.	chili powder
2		garlic cloves, finely minced
1	dash	apple cider vinegar

Stuffing

7	oz.	fresh chorizo sausage meat, finely chopped, dried chorizo is optional
1		egg
½		onion, finely diced
3		scallions, cut into rings

Mexicana Mop

Juice from 2 oranges		
½	cup	apple cider vinegar
½	cup	water
1	tbsp.	olive oil
2		garlic cloves, finely minced

Preparation:

1. The day before barbecuing, combine the rub and rub the meat well with it inside and outside. Wrap in foil and marinate overnight in the refrigerator.

2. Combine the ingredients for the salsa before barbecuing and set aside in a cool place to marinate.

3. Take the meat from the refrigerator and heat the smoker to 230° Fahrenheit [110°C].

4. Mix the stuffing well and fill into the pocket of the pork loin. Then tie the roast together with string.

5. Combine the mop ingredients and heat.

6. In a pan sear, the meat on all sides (you can use the side firebox on a barrel or offset smoker here), and place into the smoker.

7. Smoke for 2–2 ½ hours and mop every 30 minutes in the process.

8. Then spread 2 tablespoons of the mop sauce and ½ cup of the salsa over the meat, wrap tightly in aluminum foil, and place into the smoker once more for approximately one hour.

9. Cut the finished meat into slices and serve with the remaining salsa.

Caribbean Pork Neck

Caribbean, fruity—a dream come true. A touch of rum and the mango sauce make the South Sea feeling perfect.

Ingredients: **Caribbean Rub**

1	tbsp.	brown sugar
2	tsp.	allspice, ground
2	tsp.	onion powder
½	tsp.	thyme, dried
1	tsp.	salt
½	tsp.	nutmeg

Meat

5½	lbs.	pork neck
4	tbsp.	dark rum to rub the meat

Caribbean Mop

1	cup	chicken broth
½	cup	apple cider vinegar
1	cup	water
¼	cup	dark rum
2	tbsp.	olive oil

Mango Sauce

1		mango, diced into small pieces
2	tbsp.	mango chutney
½		onion, finely diced
½	cup	chicken broth
2–3	tbsp.	dark rum
2	tbsp.	coconut milk, creamy
1	tsp.	Caribbean rub
1	dash	Tabasco sauce
2	tsp.	butter

Preparation:
1. The day before barbecuing, combine the rub, and first rub the meat with the rum and then with half of the rub. Wrap in foil and marinate in the refrigerator overnight.
2. Take the meat from the refrigerator, rub again, and heat the smoker to 230° Fahrenheit [110°C].
3. Mix the mop ingredients and heat.
4. Smoke the meat for 4 ½–5 hours and mop every 30 minutes in the process.
5. Meanwhile puree the mango, onion, and chutney. Mix with the remaining ingredients, except for the butter, and let simmer for 20 minutes. Keep warm and stir in the butter only shortly before serving.
6. Cut the neck roast into slices and serve with the warm sauce.

Sweet & Spicy Pork Fillet

Honey and exotic spices provide a special taste. The pork fillet tastes best with a fruity BBQ sauce or a chutney.

Ingredients: **Sweet Sensation Rub**
Recipe, see page 74
"Stuffed Pork Loin Mexicano"

Meat

2		pork fillets

Sweet Honey Mop
Remainder of the rub above that is not necessary for rubbing

1½	cups	chicken broth
2	tbsp.	olive oil
1	tbsp.	apple cider vinegar
2	tbsp.	honey

Preparation:
1. The day before barbecuing, first apply some oil and then rub in with a couple tablespoons of the rub. Wrap in foil and marinate overnight in the refrigerator.
2. Take the fillets out of the refrigerator and heat the smoker to 230° Fahrenheit [110°C].
3. Mix the ingredients for the mop sauce and heat.
4. Sear the fillets in a pan on all sides (you can use the side firebox on a barrel or offset smoker here) and place into the smoker.
5. Smoke for 2−2 ½ hours and mop every 30 minutes in the process, the fillets are done when they have a core temperature of 160° Fahrenheit [70°C].

BEEF

Whether pork is better suited for smoking—or even tastes better—or you would rather have beef is a matter of strong opinion. In the South people swear by pork, for Texans beef is the real deal, and the truth is probably somewhere in the middle. But the fact is that we shouldn't exclude any BBQ variants. If we did, we would simply miss out on too much.

Beef first came into the smoker in pieces that were left over from carving and judged unsuitable for grilling or roasting. The classic examples for this are brisket and beef ribs.

Today fillets, roast beef, and steaks make their way into the smoker more and more often. There are numerous recipes and methods of preparation for these cuts, *fortunately...*

BRISKET

With time and the right method, even the toughest piece of meat becomes tender and enjoyable. Brisket is exactly such a piece of meat, probably one of the roughest. If you prepare it correctly, brisket is difficult to outdo in flavor and tenderness.

What Is BRISKET Anyway?

Brisket is the part of the cow underneath the chuck and is split into the point cut and flat cut. The point cut is meatier and fattier, thus best suited for BBQ. This relatively inexpensive meat has many connective tissues and must be cooked for a long time at low temperatures, similar to pulled pork. Only then does the collagen dissolve in the meat and the end result is tender and juicy.

Braggin' Rights Brisket

With this brisket you have the right to brag. This consistent, classic recipe is definitely convincing with regards to taste.

Ingredients: Wild Willy's Number 1-derful Rub

½	cup	paprika powder, sweet
¼	cup	pepper, freshly ground
¼	cup	coarse salt
¼	cup	sugar
2	tbsp.	chili powder
2	tbsp.	garlic powder
2	tbsp.	onion powder
2	tbsp.	cayenne pepper

Meat

9–11 lbs.		brisket

Basic Beer Mop

4	cups	beer
½	cup	apple cider vinegar
½	cup	water
¼	cup	olive oil
½		onion, diced
2		garlic cloves, minced
1	tbsp.	Worcester sauce
1	tbsp.	Wild Willy's number 1–derful rub (see above)

Preparation:
1. The day before barbecuing, combine the ingredients for the rub and massage the meat with it on all sides. Wrap the meat tightly in foil and let marinate overnight in the refrigerator.
2. Take the meat out of the refrigerator four hours before barbecuing and let it sit at room temperature.
3. Heat the smoker to approximately 212° Fahrenheit [100°C].
4. Mix the mop ingredients and heat over a low flame.
5. Place the meat in the smoker with the flesh side up and cook to a core temperature of 195°–205° Fahrenheit [90°C–95°C]. Thoroughly mop every 1 ½ hours.
6. After the end of the cooking time, let the meat rest for 20 minutes in aluminum foil and then separate the fattier top side from the bottom side. The cut should have a layer of fat running through it that is easy to recognize.
7. Slice both sides thinly against the grain and serve with BBQ sauce.

Brisket Express

This recipe is excellently suited for pit bosses who do not have a barrel smoker or who do not constantly want to attend to the fire. The smoky flavor comes from the smoked salt and from the bottle, and the cooking time is only five hours.

Ingredients: Express Rub

2	tbsp.	smoked salt
2	tbsp.	brown sugar
2	tbsp.	paprika powder
2	tbsp.	chili powder
2	tbsp.	black pepper, freshly ground

Meat

4–6 lbs.		brisket

Express Marinade

2	tbsp.	express rub
2	cups	beer
1		onion, finely diced
½	cup	apple cider vinegar
¼	cup	olive oil
2		chili peppers
2	tbsp.	liquid smoke

Preparation:
1. The day before barbecuing combine the rub ingredients, puree two tablespoons of the rub with the ingredients for the marinade, and rub the meat with it on all sides. Wrap tightly in foil and let marinate overnight in the refrigerator.
2. Take the meat from the refrigerator four hours before barbecuing, dry with a paper towel, and rub the meat with the remaining rub. Set aside two tablespoons of the rub.
3. Heat the smoker to approximately 212° Fahrenheit [100°C] and smoke the brisket for three hours.
4. Then sprinkle with two tablespoons of the rub and wrap in aluminum foil.
5. Cook for two more hours.
6. After the cooking time, let the brisket rest in aluminum foil for 20 minutes and then separate the fattier top side from the bottom side. The cut should have a layer of fat running through it that is easy to recognize.
7. Slice both sides thinly against the grain and serve with a smoky BBQ sauce or horseradish.

Non-Classic Brisket

This recipe probably causes frowns in Dallas. But, in *our* region you can go ahead and try it for once. Against all tradition, this brisket is placed in a brine that helps the meat become tender.

Ingredients:

Brine

½	cup	salt
6	cups	water
6	tbsp.	sugar
¼	cup	pickling spice

Meat

4–6	lbs.	brisket

Non-classic Rub

¼	cup	pepper, freshly ground
¼	cup	coriander seed, crushed
¼	cup	mustard seed, crushed
6	tbsp.	salt
2	tbsp.	garlic powder

Preparation:

1. The day before barbecuing, combine the ingredients for the brine and place the meat in it overnight in the refrigerator.

2. Take the meat out of the refrigerator four hours before barbecuing, dry with a paper towel, and let the brisket sit at room temperature for two hours.

3. Spread the rub on the meat and thoroughly massage in.

4. Heat the smoker to approximately 230° Fahrenheit [110°C] and smoke the brisket for three hours.

5. Then wrap in aluminum foil and cook for 2 more hours.

6. Let rest for 20 minutes in aluminum foil after cooking, and then separate the fattier top side from the bottom side. The cut should have a layer of fat running through it that is easy to recognize.

7. Slice both sides thinly against the grain and serve with a smoky BBQ sauce or horseradish.

Wet-Rubbed Brisket

A wet rub is the same thing as a paste. Like a paste or rub, it is applied before barbecuing. In this recipe the meat is mopped only with apple juice.

Ingredients:	Wet Rub		
	3	tbsp.	brown sugar
	2	tbsp.	paprika powder
	1	tbsp.	cayenne pepper
	1	tbsp.	salt
	1	tbsp.	onion powder
	1	tbsp.	black pepper, freshly ground
	1	tbsp.	cumin
	½	tbsp.	garlic powder
	4	tbsp.	Worcester sauce
	1	tbsp.	Tabasco sauce

	Meat		
	11–13	lbs.	brisket

Apple juice for mopping

Preparation:
1. The day before barbecuing, combine the rub ingredients and massage into the meat on all sides. Tightly wrap the meat in foil and let it marinate overnight in the refrigerator.
2. Take the meat out of the refrigerator four hours before barbecuing and let it sit at room temperature.
3. Heat the smoker to approximately 212° Fahrenheit [100°C].
4. Place the meat into the smoker with the meaty side up, and cook to a core temperature of 195°–205° Fahrenheit [90°C–95°C]. Thoroughly mop every 1½ hours.
5. After cooking, let the brisket rest in aluminum foil for 20 minutes and then separate the fattier top side from the bottom side. The cut should have a layer of fat running through it that is easy to recognize.
6. Slice both sides thinly against the grain and serve with BBQ sauce.

SPECIALS

Beef Jerky

So that you don't have to go without a snack from the smoker along the way, the cowboys invented jerky. Jerky is beef dried in the smoker that keeps for a long time and is full of flavor.

Ingredients:	Jerky Marinade		
	½	cup	Worcester sauce
	½	cup	soy sauce
	¼	cup	brown sugar
	4		garlic cloves, finely minced
	2	tsp.	black pepper, freshly ground
	2	tsp.	chili flakes
	1	tsp.	onion powder

	Meat		
	2	lbs.	thinly cut sirloin

Preparation:
1. Cut the steaks into thin strips with a very sharp knife and remove all of the fat. It is much easier if you freeze them for approximately 30 minutes.
2. Combine the ingredients for the marinade, thoroughly mix with the strips of meat, and let sit for one hour.
3. Meanwhile, heat the smoker to approximately 230° Fahrenheit [110°C].
4. Drain the strips of meat, place them next to each other on a piece of aluminum foil, and smoke for 45 minutes.
5. Now loosely seal the foil over the meat and smoke for one more hour until the meat is nicely dry.
6. Cool and serve.

Drunk and Dirty Sirloin

The obligatory bourbon recipe must naturally be present with a fillet. The recipe comes from Kentucky, the capital of bourbon.

Ingredients: **Drunk and Dirty Marinade**

1	cup	soy sauce
½	cup	water
½	cup	bourbon
¼	cup	Worcester sauce
2	tbsp.	brown sugar
½	tsp.	ginger powder
4		garlic cloves

Meat

2–3	lbs.	fillet of beef

Additional

2	tbsp.	black pepper, coarsely ground
1	tsp.	white pepper, coarsely ground
¼	cup	olive oil

Preparation:

1. The day before barbecuing, combine the ingredients for the marinade and place the meat in it overnight in the refrigerator.
2. Take the meat out of the refrigerator four hours before barbecuing, remove from the marinade, drain, and save the marinade. Dab the remaining marinade with a paper towel and rub the meat with oil. Mix the white pepper with the black pepper and spread on the fillet. Let sit at room temperature for two hours.
3. Heat the smoker to approximately 230° Fahrenheit [110°C] and smoke the fillet for 1 ¹/₂ hours.
4. In the meantime, boil the marinade and reduce to a quarter to form a sauce.
5. Serve with the warm marinade.

Quick-and-Easy Fillet

Quick and easy to prepare, swiftly smoked, and really good. The simple things are often the best.

Ingredients:

Garlic Paste

8		garlic cloves, unpeeled
1	tbsp.	coarse salt
1	tsp.	olive oil

Meat

2–3	lbs.	fillet of beef

Additional

1–2	tbsp.	black pepper, freshly ground
½	tsp.	white pepper
1½	cups	beef stock
3	tbsp.	olive oil

Preparation:

1. Cook the unpeeled garlic cloves without oil in a pan for 6–8 minutes, always stirring well in the process.
2. Peel the cloves and work into a coarse paste with the oil and salt.
3. Thoroughly rub the fillet with the paste and save one teaspoon. Mix the white pepper with the black pepper and spread over the fillet.
4. Heat the smoker to 230° Fahrenheit [110°C].
5. For the mop, mix the stock with the remaining paste and two tablespoons of olive oil and heat.
6. Sear the meat on all sides, place in the smoker for approximately 1½ hours, and mop every 20 minutes.
7. The fillet is finished at a core temperature of 135° Fahrenheit [57 °C] and pink in the center.

Mommy's Meat Loaf

There are thousands of recipes for mom's meat loaf, and each one is naturally "the best." Therefore, a recipe for a proper meatloaf must be present here.

Ingredients:

Meat Loaf

1	tbsp.	olive oil
½	cup	onions, finely diced
½		red pepper finely diced
3		garlic cloves, finely minced
1	tsp.	black pepper, freshly ground
1	tsp.	coarse salt
½	tsp.	cumin
1½	cups	bread crumbs
3	tbsp.	sour cream
2	tbsp.	Worcester sauce
1		egg
¼	cup	beef broth
1	tsp.	Tabasco sauce

Meat

3	lbs.	mixed ground meat

Basic Beer Mop

1½	cups	beer
½	cup	apple cider vinegar
½	cup	water
¼	cup	olive oil
½		onion, finely diced
2		garlic cloves, finely minced
1	tbsp.	Worcester sauce
1	tbsp.	rub according to taste
		BBQ sauce according to taste

Preparation:

1. Heat the smoker to 230° Fahrenheit [110°C].
2. Heat the oil in a pan and cook the onion, pepper, garlic, salt, pepper, and cumin together until the vegetables are soft. Cool slightly and pour into a bowl.
3. Thoroughly mix well with the other meat loaf ingredients and the meat, placing the mixture into a suitable baking dish. The mixture should fill up the dish and have the shape of a mound at the top.
4. Mix the mop ingredients and heat.
5. Place the meat loaf in the smoker and smoke for 45 minutes until the edges loosen. Then carefully lift out of the dish and continue smoking directly on the grate for 1½ hours longer. In the process mop every 20 minutes.
6. Brush with a BBQ sauce according to taste 20 minutes before the end of the cooking time.
7. Remove from the smoker and let rest for ten minutes. Cut into slices and serve warm or cold according to taste.

Smoked Sirloin

Smoked as a whole and then thinly sliced, it tastes good warm or as a cold cut. The chipotle rub provides a delicious exterior. An additional mop sauce is unnecessary because the fat layer keeps the meat juicy.

Ingredients:

Chipotle rub

2–3		dried chipotle peppers, ground
3	tbsp.	black pepper, ground
2	tbsp.	oregano, dried
1	tbsp.	coriander, dried, no seeds
1		bay leaf, ground
1	tsp.	cumin, ground
1	tsp.	onion powder
1	tsp.	orange zest, dried and ground

Meat

4	lbs.	whole roast beef

Preparation:

1. The day before barbecuing, combine the ingredients for the rub and rub the meat all over with it. Wrap in foil and let marinate overnight in the refrigerator.
2. Heat the smoker to 230° Fahrenheit [110°C] and, in the meantime, remove the meat from the refrigerator and unwrap.
3. Place the roast beef in the smoker with the meaty side up and smoke for 4–5 hours until the core temperature of 140° Fahrenheit [60°C] is reached. The meat then has a medium doneness.
4. Remove from the smoker and cut into thin slices.

Soy-Glazed Flank Steak

Flank steak is a thin cut from the lower flank, directly in front of the hind legs.

Ingredients: **Soy Marinade and Glaze**

½	cup	soy sauce
¼	cup	pickapeppa sauce, available at specialty retailers
¼	cup	Worcester sauce
¼	cup	red wine
¼	cup	red wine vinegar
3	tbsp.	brown sugar
1½	tbsp.	sesame oil
2		garlic cloves

Meat

2–4	lbs.	flank steaks

Preparation:
1. The day before barbecuing, mix the ingredients for the marinade and keep the meat in it overnight in the refrigerator.
2. Take the meat out of the refrigerator four hours before barbecuing, dry with a paper towel, and save the remaining marinade. Let the steaks sit at room temperature for two hours.
3. In the meantime, boil the marinade and reduce to half. Keep warm as the meat is glazed with it.
4. Glaze the steaks, place in the smoker, and glaze once more after 25 minutes.
5. Smoke for 45–55 minutes until the meat has reached a medium doneness.
6. Slice against the grain and serve with the remaining glaze as a sauce.

Standing Tall Prime Rib

A great look and a wonderful flavor—a standing rib roast unites both elements. It is a rib eye or entrecote on the bone that is prepared as a whole. If you split the bones in two, you get the number of portions.

Ingredients: **Standing Tall Marinade**

1½	cups	red wine
1½	cups	red wine vinegar
½	cup	olive oil
4	tsp.	rosemary, dried
4		garlic cloves, finely minced
2	tsp.	thyme, dried

Meat

4	lbs.	rib eye on the bone

Basic Black Rub

1½	tbsp.	black pepper, freshly ground
1½	tsp.	coarse salt

Preparation:
1. The day before barbecuing, combine the ingredients for the marinade and place the meat in it overnight in the refrigerator.
2. Take the meat from the refrigerator four hours before barbecuing, dry with a paper towel, and save the remaining marinade. Mix the salt with the black pepper and spread over the meat. Let sit at room temperature for two hours.
3. Heat the smoker to approximately 230° Fahrenheit [110°C] and place the rib eye on the bones, with the meaty side up, in the smoker and smoke for 2 ½ hours. The core temperature should be 140° Fahrenheit [60°C].
4. In the meantime, boil the marinade and mop the meat with it every 30 minutes.
5. Let rest for ten minutes after the end of the cooking time, remove from the bone, and cut into slices.

There need not always be large amounts of fatty or marbled meat—tender lamb, fine veal, and crispy suckling pig are also excellently suited for preparation in a smoker.

LAMB, VEAL, & CO.

Suckling Pig Loin
with Malt Beer Sauce

If you raise the temperature, you can definitely prepare a roast with a crispy crust in a smoker. An especially fine and tender version is the suckling pig loin. And yet so simple.

Ingredients:

Paste

1	bundle	marjoram, the leaves plucked off and finely chopped
½	cup	olive oil
1	tbsp.	black pepper, freshly ground

Meat

1	suckling pig loin (with rind, approximately 4 lbs.)

Additional

1	Spanish onion, diced

Malt Beer Sauce

1½	cups	malt beer
1		bay leaf
1	tbsp.	cumin
1½	cups	beef stock
1	tbsp.	cornstarch
1	tbsp.	coarse salt

Preparation:

1. The day before barbecuing, score the rind of the suckling pig loin crosswise with a sharp knife. Mix the marjoram with oil and pepper. Rub the roast on all sides with it, wrap in foil, and marinate overnight in the refrigerator.

2. Take the meat from the refrigerator and heat the smoker to 356°–392° Fahrenheit [180°C–200°C].

3. Place a drip pan of the roast's size in the smoker under the grate, pour in and distribute the onions. Place the suckling pig loin with the rind side up on the grate, salt, and smoke for approximately 1 ½ hours. In the process brush on some malt beer every 15 minutes. If the onions become too dark, add water.

4. For the sauce, pour the juices from the roast and onions into a pot. Mix the bay leaves and cumin with the remaining beer and boil down to half. Pour on the beef stock and boil down to half once more. Combine with starch and season to taste.

Peters Piglet

Fennel seed and black pepper give this leg of suckling pig a very special flavor. The mop sauce provides the necessary shine.

Ingredients: Peters Piglet Rub

2	tbsp.	fennel seed
2	tbsp.	black peppercorn
2	tsp.	chili flakes
1	tsp.	garlic powder
1½	tsp.	onion powder
1½	tsp.	marjoram, dried

Meat

1		leg of suckling pig

Additional

3	tbsp.	coarse salt

Peters Piglet Mop

1	cup	beer
½	cup	honey
½	cup	beef broth
3	tbsp.	white wine vinegar

Preparation:
1. The day before barbecuing, cut diamond patterns into the rind of the leg. Cook the fennel seed and peppercorn in an ungreased pan until they are fragrant. Then grind together and mix with the remaining rub ingredients. Thoroughly rub the leg all around, also in the cuts of the rind. Tightly wrap in foil and let marinate overnight in the refrigerator.
2. Remove the leg from the refrigerator and rub with coarse salt.
3. Heat the smoker to 356° Fahrenheit [180°C] and meanwhile mix the mop ingredients and heat.
4. Smoke the leg for 4–5 hours, mopping every 45 minutes in the process.

Racks of Lamb

Racks of lamb correspond to roast beef on the bone. They are cooked perfectly as a whole and then sliced into chops. In this recipe they are prepared in a classic way.

Ingredients: Rack Paste

5		garlic cloves, finely minced
2	tbsp.	fresh rosemary, finely chopped
2	stalks	fresh mint, finely chopped
5	tbsp.	olive oil
1	tbsp.	black pepper, freshly ground
1	tbsp.	coarse salt

Meat

2		racks of lamb, cleaned, approximately 14 oz. [400 g] each

Preparation:
1. The day before barbecuing, mix the ingredients for the paste well and thoroughly rub the racks of lamb with it. Cover and marinate overnight in the refrigerator.
2. Heat the smoker to 248° Fahrenheit [120°C] and in the meantime dab the marinade remnants from the racks of lamb and sear the meat in a pan all over.
3. Place the racks in the smoker with the bones up leaning against each other and cook for approximately 30–40 minutes. A core temperature of 135° Fahrenheit [57°C] should not be exceeded.
4. Remove the meat from the smoker and let it rest in aluminum foil for five minutes. Then cut into slices, each with a bone.

Martini Leg of Lamb

Martini, neither shaken nor stirred, makes this leg of lamb something extraordinary.

Ingredients:

Martini Paste

½		onion, diced
10		garlic cloves
		lime juice and zest
3	tbsp.	gin
2	tbsp.	salt
¼	cup	olive oil

Meat

1		leg of lamb

Martini Mop

1	cup	gin
1	cup	beef broth
½	cup	water
3	tbsp.	lime juice
2	tbsp.	olive oil

Preparation:

1. The day before barbecuing, mix the ingredients for the paste and thoroughly brush the lamb with it. Wrap it in foil and let marinate overnight in the refrigerator.

2. Remove the leg from the refrigerator and let it sit for 30 minutes.

3. Heat the smoker to 356° Fahrenheit [180°C] and in the meantime mix the mop ingredients and heat.

4. Smoke the leg of lamb for 2–3 hours until a core temperature of 140° Fahrenheit [60°C] is reached. Mop every 30 minutes in the process.

5. Remove from the smoker and let rest for ten minutes.

Sage-Madeira Veal Knuckle

Few pieces change their appearance in the smoker as much as veal knuckle. The previously hardly visible bone sticks out of the meat up to 4″ [10 cm] after cooking. Wonderful.

Ingredients:	Sage Paste		
	1	cup	fresh sage leaves
	4		garlic cloves
	¼	tsp.	salt
	2	tbsp.	Madeira
	2	tbsp.	lime juice
	5	tbsp.	olive oil
	Meat		
	1		veal knuckle
	Additional		
	5	slices	bacon
	Madeira Mop		
	¾	cup	Madeira
	2	tbsp.	lime juice
	½	cup	water
	1½	tbsp.	olive oil

Preparation:
1. The day before barbecuing, chop up the ingredients for the paste with a hand blender and add the oil. Thoroughly brush the knuckle with it, wrap in foil, and marinate in the refrigerator overnight.
2. Heat the smoker to 320° Fahrenheit [160°C] and in the meantime mix the mop ingredients and heat.
3. Place the veal knuckle in the smoker and cover with the slices of bacon.
4. Smoke for 3–4 hours until a core temperature of 140° Fahrenheit [60°C] is reached and mop every 30 minutes in the process.
5. Remove from the smoker and let rest for ten minutes.

Veal Knuckle with Spring Vegetables

For this veal knuckle, which is cooked in a baking dish, the side dish is directly next to it. The smoker is heated to 320° Fahrenheit [160°C], so it has a significantly higher temperature compared to most other recipes.

Ingredients:	Rub		
	1	tbsp.	rosemary, dried
	1	tbsp.	thyme, dried
	½	tbsp.	chili flakes
	½	tbsp.	brown sugar
	Meat		
	1–2		veal knuckles, trimmed
	Beer Mop		
	2	cups	dark beer
	1	tbsp.	thyme, dried
	2–3	sprigs	rosemary
	2	tbsp.	Worcester sauce
	1	tbsp.	black pepper, freshly ground
	1	tbsp.	coarse salt
	Vegetables		
	4–6		potatoes, unpeeled, halved
	6		whole yellow cherry tomatoes
	6		whole red cherry tomatoes
	6		whole scallions, cleaned
	6		small carrots, peeled
	2	tbsp.	celeriac, finely chopped

Preparation:

1. The day before barbecuing, mix the ingredients for the rub and thoroughly rub the knuckles with it. Wrap in foil and let marinate overnight in the refrigerator.

2. Remove from the refrigerator, unwrap, and heat the smoker to 320° Fahrenheit [160°C].

3. In the meantime, combine the ingredients for the mop sauce and pour into a baking dish.

4. Place the meat into the sauce and spread the vegetables around.

5. Loosely cover with aluminum foil and smoke for one hour. Then remove the foil and smoke an additional hour.

6. Now thoroughly brush with the mop sauce every 15 minutes. In the process, also pour the sauce over the vegetables.

7. After cooking, let rest, covered for ten minutes, and serve with the vegetables as a side dish.

Stuffed Saddle of Veal

Next to the fillet, the tender saddle is the best from the calf. And with this stuffing, it will be refined once again.

Ingredients: **Cheryl's Cider Soak**

1½	cups	apple juice or cider
½	cup	apple cider vinegar
½		onion, diced
1½	tbsp.	Worcester sauce
1	tbsp.	olive oil
1	tsp.	cinnamon
1	tsp.	thyme, dried

Meat

4½	lbs.	whole saddle of veal, without bones and with a pocket cut in for the stuffing

Stuffing

2	slices	bacon, cut into small pieces
½		apple, such as Granny Smith
2	tbsp.	onions, finely diced
1		garlic clove, finely minced
7	oz.	ground veal
¼	cup	bread crumbs
3		dates, pitted
3		scallions, cut into fine rings
2	tbsp.	fresh parsley, chopped
½	tsp.	rosemary, dried
1	pinch	cinnamon

Preparation:
1. The day before barbecuing, mix the ingredients for the soak and place the meat in it, working some into the pocket in the process. Marinate in the refrigerator overnight.
2. Remove the meat from the marinade and dab. Boil the remaining marinade and keep warm.
3. Heat the smoker to 248° Fahrenheit [120°C] and let the meat rest during this time.
4. For the stuffing, render the bacon and cook the apple, onion, and garlic in the fat until soft.
5. Mix with the remaining ingredients and fill the saddle of veal with it.
6. In a pan, sear the meat on all sides and then smoke for two hours, mopping with the remaining marinade every 20–30 minutes.
7. Let rest for ten minutes and serve in slices.

Veal Loin, Whole and Pure

Here, less is more. The tender veal gets sufficient flavor from the bone and the subtle smoke. Too many spices would quickly interfere with the fine taste.

Ingredients:

2	tbsp.	fresh thyme, sage, or rosemary
1	tbsp.	black pepper, coarsely ground
1	tbsp.	coarse salt
4	tbsp.	olive oil

Meat

1		whole veal loin, 7 rib bones, approximately 5½ lbs.

Preparation:
1. The day before barbecuing, mix the ingredients for the paste well and thoroughly rub the entire veal loin with it. Cover and marinate overnight in the refrigerator.
2. Heat the smoker to 230° Fahrenheit [110°C] and wrap the bones with aluminum foil so that they do not turn black from the smoke.
3. Cook for approximately 2 ½ hours. In the process, a core temperature of 135° Fahrenheit [57°C] should not be exceeded.
4. Remove from the smoker and let rest in aluminum foil for five minutes. Then slice the loin into individual chops.

POULTRY

Poultry easily becomes dry on the grill. It is certainly very popular among health-conscious people because of its low fat content, but during preparation you must be on your guard ... or use a smoker.

This version of BBQ has long been established because the slow cooking process in the smoker is ideal for chicken and other types of poultry, and refined with the right rub and a good BBQ sauce.

But if you look forward to the crispy skin of a roast chicken, you will be disappointed because, prepared at low temperatures in the smoker, the skin does not become crispy.

BBC – Beer Butt Chicken

Beer Butt Chicken is an absolute classic. During its preparation, an entire chicken is cooked without grate contact.

Ingredients: **Wild Willy's Number 1-derful Rub**

½	cup	paprika powder, sweet
¼	cup	pepper, freshly ground
¼	cup	coarse salt
¼	cup	sugar
2	tbsp.	chili powder
2	tbsp.	garlic powder
2	tbsp.	onion powder
2	tbsp.	cayenne pepper

Injection

1½	cups	beer
¼	cup	olive oil
¼	cup	apple cider vinegar
2	tsp.	Wild Willy's Number 1–derful Rub

Meat

2		chickens approximately 2½ lbs. each

Mop

1½	cups	beer
1	cup	chicken broth
¼	cup	olive oil
½	cup	water
1	tsp.	Wild Willy's Number 1–derful Rub
½		onion, diced
¼	cup	apple cider vinegar
4		garlic cloves, finely minced
2	10 fl.oz.	cans beer or equivalent chicken holder

Preparation:

1. The day before barbecuing, mix the ingredients for the rub, inject, and clean the chickens.
2. With a marinade injector, inject half a cup of the injection deeply at multiple locations in the breast and legs and then thoroughly rub the chicken with the remainder of the liquid.
3. Then massage well with the rub, and save one tablespoon of the rub. Pack the chickens in plastic bags and marinate overnight in the refrigerator.
4. Remove the chickens from the refrigerator and heat the smoker to 230° Fahrenheit [110°C]. Meanwhile empty the beer cans halfway and remove the lid with a can opener. Spread half of the onion, vinegar, and garlic as well as the remaining rub on the cans and set the chickens on the cans.
5. It is best to place the chicken on a plate in the smoker and smoke for approximately four hours.
6. Mix the ingredients for the mop, heat, and mop the chickens with it every 30 minutes.
7. After cooking, remove the chickens from the smoker, remove the skin, carve up, and serve with a good BBQ sauce according to taste.

Mustard-Lime Chicken

In addition to the classic version, Beer Butt Chicken, there are naturally many possibilities to prepare entire chickens in the smoker—for example, this recipe with limes and mustard. The rub provides the necessary seasoning.

Ingredients:

Poultry Perfect Rub

6	tbsp.	paprika powder, sweet
2	tbsp.	black pepper, freshly ground
2	tbsp.	celery salt
2	tbsp.	sugar
1	tbsp.	garlic powder
1	tbsp.	mustard powder
1	tsp.	cayenne pepper
		zest from two limes

Meat

2		chickens approximately 2½ lbs. each

For the Stuffing

2	tbsp.	butter
1	tbsp.	Worcester sauce
1		onion, sliced into thin rings
1		lime, divided into eight pieces

Lemon Splash

1½	cups	chicken broth
½	cup	lime juice
½	cup	water
½		onion, diced
½	cup	butter
1	tbsp.	Worcester sauce
1	tbsp.	mustard
2	tsp.	Poultry Perfect Rub

Preparation:

1. The day before barbecuing, mix the ingredients for the rub and clean the chickens.
2. Melt the butter and stir in the Worcester sauce. Rub the chickens inside and out with this mixture. Then massage with the rub, save one third.
3. Pack the chickens in plastic bags and marinate overnight in the refrigerator.
4. Take the chickens from the refrigerator the next day and heat the smoker to 230° Fahrenheit [110°C]. Meanwhile rub the chickens once more and again keep two tablespoons of the rub. Then place the onion rings and the lime wedges into the chickens.
5. Mix the ingredients for the mop (Lemon Splash) and heat.
6. Place the chickens into the smoker with the breast down and smoke for four hours. Mop every 30 minutes and after half of the cooking time turn onto their backs.
7. After cooking, remove the chickens from the smoker, remove the skin, carve up, and serve with a BBQ or mustard sauce according to taste.

Cheese Chicken

Creamy sheep's milk cheese under the chicken skin provides flavor and keeps the meat extra juicy.

Ingredients:

Paste

3½	oz.	cream cheese from sheep's milk or goat milk
1	tbsp.	pesto
8–10	leaves	basil

Meat

1		chicken approximately 2½ lbs.

Fancy Mop

1	cup	chicken broth
½	cup	white wine
½	cup	water
2	tbsp.	olive oil
1	tbsp.	pesto

Preparation:

1. The day before barbecuing, mix the sheep's milk cheese with the pesto and clean the chicken.
2. Spread the cheese mixture inside, outside, and under the skin without damaging it. Spread the basil leaves on the chicken under the skin.
3. Pack the chicken in a plastic bag and marinate overnight in the refrigerator.
4. The following day remove the chicken from the refrigerator and heat the smoker to 230° Fahrenheit [110°C].
5. Mix the ingredients for the mop and heat.
6. Place the chicken into the smoker with the breast down and smoke for four hours. Mop every 30 minutes and turn on its back after half of the cooking time.
7. After cooking, remove the chicken from the smoker, remove the skin, carve up, and serve with a BBQ sauce according to taste.

Quick Chick

No time to prepare an entire chicken? No problem. You will also get great results smoking chicken breast. The mop also helps keep the chicken from drying out, and everything left over goes on to a sandwich the next day.

Ingredients:

Split Second Dry Rub

1	tbsp.	paprika powder, sweet
1	tsp.	coarse salt
1	tsp.	sugar
½	tsp.	black pepper, freshly ground
½	tsp.	onion powder
1	pinch	cayenne pepper

Meat

6		individual chicken breast fillets, without skin

Split Second Mop

1	cup	orange juice
3	tbsp.	butter
1	tbsp.	Worcester sauce

Preparation:

1. Heat the smoker to 230° Fahrenheit [110°C]. Meanwhile mix the ingredients for the rub and massage the meat with it.
2. Heat the mop ingredients in a pot until the butter is melted and keep warm.
3. Drizzle the chicken breasts with one third of the mop sauce and place in the smoker.
4. Smoke for 30 minutes, turning over once, and mopping twice.

Garlic-Oregano Chicken

Garlic and chicken go very well with each other. If you add some oregano, the Italian trio is complete.

Ingredients: Oregano Marinade

2	cups	olive oil
1	cup	lime juice
6–8		garlic cloves
2	tsp.	salt
¼	cup	fresh oregano, chopped

Meat

4	entire	chicken breasts with skin and bone

Preparation:
1. The day before barbecuing, mix and puree the ingredients for the marinade. Place the chicken pieces in it and keep cold overnight.
2. The following day remove the meat from the refrigerator and heat the smoker to 230° Fahrenheit [110°C].
3. Place the chicken in the smoker with the skin side up and smoke for approximately one hour. The meat is cooked when you stick in a toothpick and the juice that comes out is clear.

Thunder Thighs

Like many pit masters of the South, the paste and mop for this recipe have African roots.

Ingredients: Thunder Paste

1		onion, coarsely diced
½	cup	orange juice
2	tbsp.	peanut butter
1	tbsp.	peanut oil
2	tsp.	anise, ground
1	tsp.	curry
1	tsp.	salt
1	tsp.	brown sugar
½	tsp.	cinnamon

Meat

6		chicken leg quarters

Thunder Mop

1	cup	chicken broth
½	cup	orange juice
¼	cup	water
1	tbsp.	peanut oil
½	tsp.	curry

Preparation:
1. The day before barbecuing, mix all ingredients for the paste with a hand blender and thickly rub the paste on the chicken legs. Pack in a bag and let marinate overnight in the refrigerator.
2. The following day, remove the meat from the refrigerator and heat the smoker to 230° Fahrenheit [110°C].
3. Heat the mop ingredients in a pot and keep warm.
4. Place the meat in the smoker and cook for approximately $1\frac{1}{2}$ hours. The legs are done when you stick a toothpick in and the juice that comes out is clear.

Delicious Drumsticks

Drumsticks are the lower legs of the chicken. And by "delicious" we mean *absolutely delicious* ... The lactic acid in the buttermilk helps to make the meat tender.

Ingredients: Delicious Marinade

1	cup	buttermilk
1	cup	fresh mint, finely chopped
¼	cup	bourbon

Meat

8		chicken leg quarters

Delicious Mop

Remaining Marinade

¼	cup	bourbon
¼	cup	water
2	tbsp.	olive oil

Preparation:
1. The day before barbecuing, mix all ingredients for the marinade and place the meat in it. Let marinate overnight in the refrigerator.
2. The following day, remove the meat from the marinade, save the marinade, and heat the smoker to 230° Fahrenheit [110°C].
3. Mix the mop ingredients and the remaining marinade, bring to a boil, and keep warm.
4. Place the meat in the smoker and cook for approximately 1 ½ hours. The legs are cooked when you stick in a toothpick and the juices that come out are clear.

Worth-the-Wait Turkey

This recipe is definitely more work, but it is worth it. And if you would like to really spoil your guests, it is exactly the right thing.

Ingredients: Injection

½	cup	garlic oil
½	cup	beer
½	tsp.	cayenne pepper

Meat

1		turkey, 11–13 lbs.

Turkey Paste

4		garlic cloves
1	tbsp.	black pepper, freshly ground
1	tbsp.	coarse salt
½	tsp.	cayenne pepper
1	tbsp.	garlic oil

Turkey Mop

2	cups	chicken broth
1	cup	beer
1	cup	water
¼	cup	olive oil

Preparation:
1. The day before barbecuing, mix the ingredients for the injection and inject deeply into different spots of the meat. In doing so, most of the liquid will get into the breast.
2. In a mortar, first crush the dry ingredients of the paste and then combine into a spreadable mixture with the oil.
3. Rub the turkey with the mixture and let marinate overnight in a large plastic bag in the refrigerator.
4. The following day take the meat out of the refrigerator and heat the smoker to 230° Fahrenheit [110 °C].
5. Wrap the turkey in a correspondingly big, damp linen cloth and tie up the ends. Then place in the smoker with the breast side down and smoke for approximately three hours per pound. In the process sprinkle the cloth every 30 minutes with some water.
6. Carefully remove the linen cloth after six hours, cut if necessary, and place the turkey on its back.
7. Heat the ingredients for the mop and mop the turkey every 30 minutes.
8. When the meat has reached a core temperature of 176° Fahrenheit [80°C], it is done and can be taken from the smoker.

Smoked Peking Duck

Ducks have so much fat under their skin that you must loosen and remove it before smoking. This procedure happens with boiling water that is poured over the duck breast.

Ingredients:

Peking Glaze

½	cup	orange juice
5	tbsp.	honey
3	tbsp.	red wine vinegar
3	tbsp.	sherry
2	tbsp.	soy sauce
½	tbsp.	black pepper, freshly ground

Meat

1	duck, 4–6½ lbs.

Stuffing

1	onion, divided into eight pieces
1	orange, divided into eight pieces

Preparation:

1. Mix the ingredients for the glaze well, boil, and let cool.
2. Meanwhile poke the duck multiple times in the breast and slowly pour over 3–4 quarts of boiling water. Thus, the fat can melt and flow out through the holes.
3. Dab the duck, rub with the glaze inside and out, and let dry.
4. In the meantime, heat the smoker to 230° Fahrenheit [110°C].
5. Place the orange and onion wedges into the duck and then set in the smoker with the breast up.
6. Smoke for approximately three hours until the core temperature is 140° Fahrenheit [60°C]. In the process, glaze every 30 minutes.
7. Serve with the remaining sauce.

FISH

Fish is healthy, delicious, and therefore offers a welcome and easy change from the usual dishes from the smoker that are often very heavy on the fat and meat. The considerably shorter cooking time, in contrast to pulled pork or brisket, allows a dinner with fish to be smoked during the week after work. Also, it is no problem to cook fish and meat at the same time in a smoker. There is no aroma transfer from the smoke.

Double Rub Salmon

For this salmon recipe you will need two different rubs. The first has the effect of a marinade and pulls the protein molecules on the surface that act as a protective layer and keep in the juices. For the second rub it is refreshed once more with a slightly modified recipe.

Ingredients: **Rub Number 1**

1	cup	brown sugar
1	cup	sea salt
3	tbsp.	garlic powder
3	tbsp.	onion powder
3	tbsp.	fresh dill, chopped
1	tbsp.	savory, dried
2	tsp.	tarragon, dried

Rub Number 2

¼	cup	brown sugar
1	tbsp.	garlic powder
1	tbsp.	onion powder
1	tsp.	savory, dried
1	tsp.	tarragon, dried

Fish

1		salmon fillet with skin, approximately 4 lbs., trimmed

Preparation:
1. Separate from each other, mix the ingredients for both rubs well and set Rub Number 2 aside.
2. Completely spread Rub Number 1 on the meaty side, then tightly wrap the fish in saran wrap, and place in the refrigerator for 3–4 hours.
3. Then carefully wash off Rub Number 1 under running water and dab the fish with paper towels. Let dry for 30 minutes until the surface is slightly sticky.
4. Heat the smoker to 230° Fahrenheit [110°C] and spread Rub Number 2 on the flesh side.
5. Place the fish in the smoker on a correspondingly big piece of aluminum foil and smoke for approximately one hour. The fish should still be slightly translucent in the center.
6. Loosely cover with some aluminum foil and let rest for five minutes.

Jamaican Jerk Salmon

Jerk is a mixture of exotic spices and belongs to the classics. The piquant flavor is specially designed for this recipe to not interfere with the fine fish flavor.

Ingredients: **Jerk Rub**

1	tbsp.	onion powder
1	tbsp.	fried onions
1	tsp.	allspice, ground
1	tsp.	black pepper, freshly ground
1	tsp.	cayenne pepper
1	tsp.	sugar
1	tsp.	thyme, dried
1	tsp.	cinnamon
1	tsp.	nutmeg
1	pinch	chili powder

Fish

1		salmon fillet with skin, approximately 4½ lbs., trimmed

Jamaican BBQ Sauce

1	cup	fish stock
2	tbsp.	honey
1	tbsp.	tamarind paste
1	tbsp.	ginger, grated
1	tbsp.	Jerk Rub

Preparation:
1. Mix the ingredients for the Jerk Rub well and apply abundant rub on the salmon fillet on the meaty side. Save one tablespoon of the rub.
2. Wrap the fish in foil and keep cold for 1–2 hours. Meanwhile heat the smoker to 230° Fahrenheit [110°C].
3. Mix the sauce ingredients, boil, and reduce to one third.
4. Unwrap the salmon, place in the smoker on a correspondingly large piece of aluminum foil, and smoke for approximately one hour.
5. Glaze after 30 minutes with the sauce and serve with the remaining sauce after the end of the cooking time.

Vodka-Brined Salmon

This salmon is placed into a brine. It sinks deeply into the fish and makes it soft and tender. Vodka gives it its special flavor.

Ingredients: Brine

¼	cup	vodka
½	cup	brown sugar
3	tbsp.	coarse salt
2	tbsp.	pickling spice
1	tsp.	dill seed

Fish

1		salmon fillet with skin, approximately 4½ lbs., trimmed

Preparation:

1. Mix all ingredients for the brine well and pour into a plastic bag. Add the salmon fillet and coat everywhere with the brine. Place in the refrigerator for 3–6 hours, according to desired intensity.
2. Heat the smoker to 230° Fahrenheit [110°C], take the fish out of the bag, and slightly dab with paper towels. The remaining spices and herbs must not be removed.
3. Place the fish in the smoker on a correspondingly large piece of aluminum foil and smoke for approximately one hour. The fish should still be slightly translucent in the center.
4. Loosely cover with aluminum foil and let rest for five minutes.

Minted Salmon Trout

Mint can be combined in many ways and it also goes very well with salmon trout. Mop only with peppermint tea here.

Ingredients: Mint Paste

½	cup	fresh mint
¼	cup	coarse salt
¼	cup	sugar
2	tbsp.	black pepper, coarsely ground
2	tbsp.	lime juice
1	tbsp.	olive oil

Fish

Approx. 2 lbs.		salmon trout fillets with skin, trimmed

Mint Mop

1	cup	peppermint tea

Preparation:

1. The day before barbecuing, mix the ingredients for the paste, puree with a hand blender, brush the fillets on the skin side with it. Wrap in Saran Wrap and marinate overnight in the refrigerator.
2. Heat the smoker to 230° Fahrenheit [110°C], unwrap the fillets, and let sit for 20 minutes.
3. Place in the smoker on a correspondingly large piece of aluminum foil and thoroughly drizzle with tea.
4. Smoke for 30–45 minutes according to the thickness of the fillets, drizzle with tea once more shortly before serving.

Salmon Fillet
from the Cedar Plank

This salmon is prepared on a wood plank. Before placing the fish onto the plank it is pre-heated. Thus there is a fine smoky flavor, even in bullet smokers without chips or chunks. When served, the entire thing is naturally an eye catcher.

Ingredients: Vinaigrette

2	tbsp.	lime juice
2	tbsp.	white balsamic
2	tbsp.	Dijon mustard
2	tbsp.	honey
2	tbsp.	chives, chopped
1	tsp.	salt
½	tsp.	granulated garlic
½	tsp.	black pepper, ground
¼	tsp.	cayenne pepper
2	fl.oz.	olive oil

Fish

1	salmon fillet with skin, approximately 3 lbs.
2	limes, cut into halves
1	cedar plank, soaked at least two hours
	pepper
	salt

Preparation:

1. Mix all ingredients except the oil for the vinaigrette and slowly add the oil. In the process beat the oil and the other ingredients with a whisk to form an emulsion.

2. Trim the salmon fillet and in portions cut to the skin. Season with pepper and salt and spread the vinaigrette on the meaty side and into the cuts.

3. Place a lime half into each cut.

4. Pre-heat the plank for approximately five minutes over direct, high heat. You can also do this with a side firebox or also with a blowtorch or the like.

5. Then set the plank into the smoker, place the entire salmon fillet on the plank, and smoke for approximately one hour. The fish should still be slightly translucent in the center.

6. Because the fish is already pre-portioned, the single pieces can be easily lifted from the skin and served.

Trout Wrapped in Bacon

The coating of bacon certainly provides flavor, but above all it protects the fish from drying out.

Ingredients: **Paste**

4		garlic cloves
2	tbsp.	lime juice
1	tsp.	Worcester sauce
1	tsp.	black pepper, freshly ground
½	tsp.	coarse salt
1	tbsp.	vegetable oil

Fish & Meat

4	whole	trout, approximately 10½ oz. each
8	slices	bacon

Stuffing

1		onion, finely diced
½		red pepper, finely diced
½		green pepper, finely diced
1	rib	celery, finely diced
16		saltine crackers, crushed
6	tbsp.	pecans, finely chopped

Preparation:
1. Crush the ingredients for the paste into small pieces in a mortar and mix until a paste forms. Rub the fish inside and out with it.
2. Heat the smoker to 230° Fahrenheit [110 °C].
3. Meanwhile render the bacon in a pan but do not fry to a crisp.
4. In the rendered fat, fry the peppers, celery, and onion until they are soft. Then remove from the stove and let cool.
5. Then add the pecans and the crushed crackers and mix.
6. Fill the fish with the mixture and then wrap each with two slices of bacon. Possibly fix with a toothpick.
7. Place in the smoker on the stomach, smoke for 40–50 minutes, and immediately serve. If the fish cannot stand on their own, you can make a corresponding holder from aluminum foil.

Aotearoa Tuna Steak

In the Maori language, Aotearoa is the name for New Zealand. This recipe has wandered many paths over the Pacific islands and has been modified here and there. The ingredients can vary, but one thing remains the same: the tuna must be of the highest quality.

Ingredients: **Marinade**

5	tbsp.	butter
5	tbsp.	sesame oil
5	tbsp.	white balsamic
2	tbsp.	lime juice
1	tsp.	ginger, grated
½	tsp.	thyme, dried
1		garlic clove, finely minced
½	tsp.	chili flakes

Fish

4		tuna steaks, 1" thick

Additional

½	tsp.	coarse salt
		soy sauce

Preparation:
1. Mix the ingredients for the marinade, rub the steaks with it all over, and let sit for one hour.
2. Heat the smoker to 230° Fahrenheit [110°C].
3. Pour the salt into a hot pan and sear the drained tuna shortly on both sides.
4. Place in the smoker and smoke for 20–25 minutes, the steaks should still be almost rare on the inside.
5. Serve with soy sauce.

Smoked Oysters

You either love them or hate them ... There is only one way to figure out your personal preference towards oysters ... you must try them.

Ingredients: Marinade & Mop

½	cup	shellfish stock
2	tbsp.	lime juice
2	tbsp.	olive oil
1	tsp.	black pepper, coarsely ground
3		garlic cloves, minced

Shellfish

| 1 | dozen | oysters |

Additional

| 20 | | ice cubes |

Preparation:
1. Shuck the oysters, in the process saving the bottom shells and the juice.
2. Mix all ingredients for the marinade with the juice from the oysters, pour in the shellfish, and keep cold for one hour.
3. Heat the smoker to 230° Fahrenheit [110°C]. Drain the shellfish meat. In the process, collect the marinade, boil, and keep warm. Place the shucked shellfish loosely into the bottom shells.
4. Put the ice cubes into a baking dish and put in the shellfish.
5. Smoke for 40 minutes and drizzle once or twice with the marinade in the process.

Smoked Scallops

This fine shellfish doesn't need much. But from the equally fine Parma ham, a wonderful flavor is added.

Ingredients: Brine

5	cups	water
¼	cup	salt
¼	cup	sugar

Shellfish & Meat

| 116 | | scallops, shucked, without coral |
| 8 | slices | Parma ham |

Additional

| 4 | | scallions, finely chopped |

Preparation:
1. Mix the ingredients for the brine and make sure that the salt and sugar completely dissolve. Add the shellfish for one hour.
2. Heat the smoker to 230° Fahrenheit [110°C]. Meanwhile, remove the shellfish from the brine and let drain on a wire rack.
3. Halve the Parma ham lengthwise, wrap around the shellfish, and fix with a toothpick.
4. Place in the smoker on a drip pan, sprinkle with the scallions, and smoke for 20 minutes.

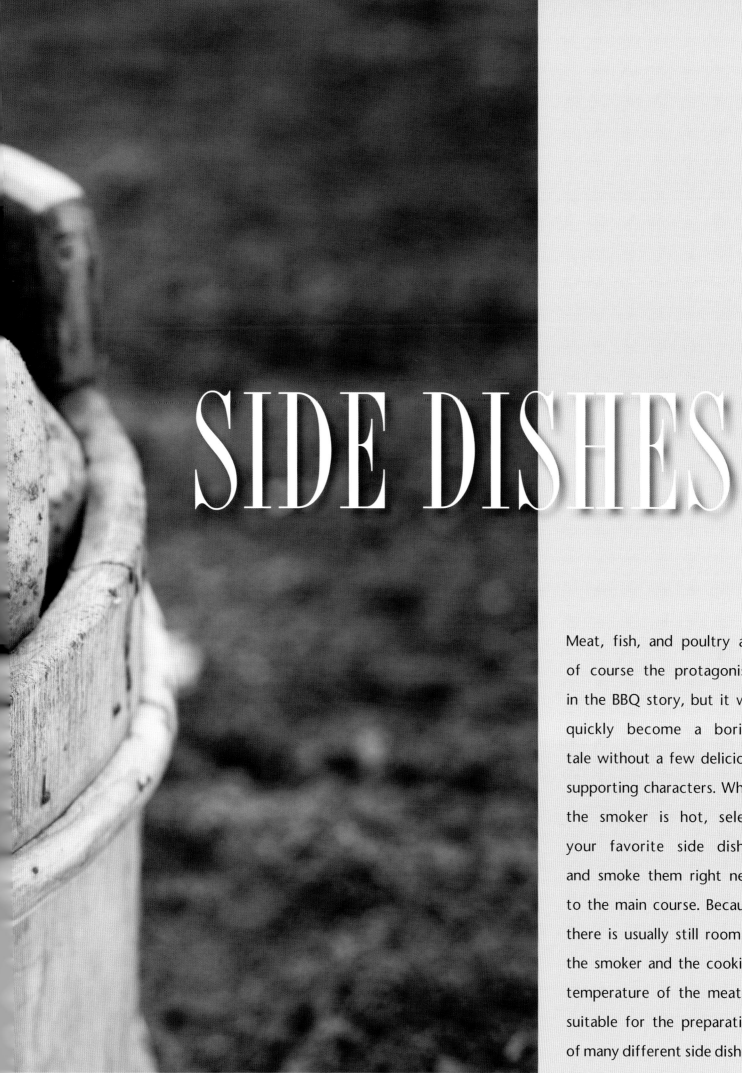

SIDE DISHES

Meat, fish, and poultry are of course the protagonists in the BBQ story, but it will quickly become a boring tale without a few delicious supporting characters. While the smoker is hot, select your favorite side dishes and smoke them right next to the main course. Because there is usually still room in the smoker and the cooking temperature of the meat is suitable for the preparation of many different side dishes.

Sweet Baked Beans

Baked beans are inexpensive, delicious, and very filling. So it's no wonder that they have a lot of followers. This recipe has a sweet flavor and goes especially well with piquant main dishes.

Ingredients:	4½	lbs.	canned baked beans
	1½	cups	BBQ sauce according to taste
	½		onion, diced
	½		green pepper, diced
	2	ribs	celery, diced
	8	tbsp.	mustard
	500	g	brown sugar
	2	tbsp.	smoked salt
	2	tbsp.	celery salt

Meat

	1	lb.	smoked bacon, diced
			You can also replace the bacon with pulled pork or brisket that is left over from the last BBQ.

Preparation:	1.	Pour all ingredients into a baking dish (approximately 8" x 12") and mix well.
	2.	Coat with brown sugar. This layer can be ¹/₃" and thicker. Do not stir.
	3.	Smoke at 230° Fahrenheit [110°C] for three hours until the sugar has dissolved and is no longer visible. Do not stir during smoking.

Corned Beef Stew

Whether you stew it directly in the smoker or classically on the side firebox in a heavy pot—this stew will not only make you satisfied but also happy. The meat is cooked very tender and therefore this stew is an excellent side dish to add to meat.

Ingredients:	1	cup	BBQ sauce according to taste
	3	cups	water
	6		potatoes, diced
	6		carrots, diced
	¼	bulb	celery, diced
	1		onion, divided into eight pieces
	3	tbsp.	flour, dissolved in 1/4 cup water
	1	tsp.	chili powder
			salt and pepper to season, to taste

Meat

	2		cans of corned beef, 12 oz. each

Preparation:	1.	Chop up the corned beef and mix with the BBQ sauce.
	2.	Add the water and chili powder and let simmer in a pot on the side firebox or in the smoker at 230° Fahrenheit [110 °C] covered for one hour.
	3.	Mix in the vegetables and cook for another hour until soft. At the end of the cooking time, dissolve the flour in the water and combine the stew with it.
	4.	Season to taste with salt and pepper and serve.

Cowboy Beans

After a hard day on the prairie these beans are exactly the right thing. Even if the workplace of many city cowboys mostly looks different today, the Cowboy Beans have not changed.

Ingredients:	1	lb.	canned kidney beans
	7	oz.	smoked bacon, diced
	2		onions, diced
	1	can	peeled tomatoes, coarsely diced
	1	tbsp.	chili powder
	1	cup	water
	2	tbsp.	Worcester sauce
	2	tbsp.	brown sugar
	1	tbsp.	mustard
	1	tsp.	salt

Preparation:
1. Render the bacon and simmer all ingredients, except for the salt, with the bacon and rendered fat in a pot on the side firebox or in the smoker at 230° Fahrenheit [110°C] covered for two hours. Occasionally stir.
2. When the beans are soft and there is too much liquid in the pot, continue cooking everything for 20 more minutes without a lid.
3. If the beans, despite the bacon, are still not spicy enough season to taste with salt.

Stuffed Onions

The size of the onions determines if this is a side dish or main dish. Spanish onions are well suited as a main dish, small red onions are used for preparing a side dish. And this recipe describes a balance.

Ingredients:	4		medium size onions
	1	tbsp.	butter
	2		garlic cloves, finely minced
	½	lb.	leaf spinach
	1½	cups	cooked rice
	3½	oz.	cooked ham, finely diced
	1	cup	bread crumbs
	6	tbsp.	grated Parmesan
	½	tsp.	thyme, dried
	½	cup	chicken broth
	1		egg, whipped
			salt and pepper, season to taste
			oil

Preparation:	1.	Halve the unpeeled onions horizontally, hollow out, and leave an edge of approximately $1/3$″.
	2.	Place into the smoker without aluminum foil or pan and smoke for 30–35 minutes at 230° Fahrenheit [110°C] until they are soft.
	3.	In the meantime heat the butter, finely chop half of the hollowed-out insides of the onions and cook with the garlic in a pan for 1–2 minutes.
	4.	Add the spinach, let wilt, and possibly add water if the spinach becomes too tough.
	5.	Mix in the remaining ingredients except for the egg. At the very end add the whipped egg and also stir in.
	6.	Remove the onions from the smoker, peel, and fill with the mixture. Sprinkle with some Parmesan and smoke for an additional 20–25 minutes.

Prince Mushroom Burger

Mushrooms must simply be present at BBQs. This dish is also well suited for vegetarians.

Ingredients:	4		very large prince mushrooms, stalks removed
	4	slices	Manchego, Bergkäse, or Gruyère
	½	cup	mayonnaise
	3	tbsp.	green pesto
	4		mini pitas, sliced and toasted
	1		large tomato, cut in slices
			olive oil
	½	tsp.	salt
	½	tsp.	black pepper, freshly ground

Preparation:	1.	Brush the mushrooms with oil, lightly salt, and smoke for approximately 20 minutes at 230° Fahrenheit [110°C] until they are soft. Place the cheese on top of the mushrooms and smoke for five more minutes.
	2.	Mix the mayonnaise, pepper, and pesto, spread on the bottom bread halves, and add a tomato slice on top of each.
	3.	Place the mushrooms on top of the tomatoes, cover with the second bread half, and serve immediately.

Tequila Sweet Potato Mash

Sweet potatoes from the South and tequila from the West are wonderfully complementary and provide a perfect combination.

Ingredients:	2	oz.	butter
	1	lb.	sweet potatoes, grated
	2½	tbsp.	brown sugar
	½	tsp.	salt
	¼	cup	tequila
	6	tbsp.	lime juice

Preparation:
1. Melt the butter in a heat-resistant dish. Stir in the sweet potatoes and evenly press down firmly on the bottom.
2. Sprinkle the brown sugar and salt over it.
3. Place the dish into the smoker and smoke at 230° Fahrenheit [110°C] for one hour. Then stir in three tablespoons of tequila and three tablespoons of lime juice. Press flat once again and smoke an additional hour.
4. Remove from the smoker, stir in the rest of the tequila and lime juice, and serve warm.

Wrapped Corn

Corn on the cob not only looks good, but it tastes great. And at a proper southern BBQ, it is an essential side dish.

Ingredients:	6		ears of corn
	6	slices	bacon
	6	tbsp.	butter
			salt and pepper to season to taste

Preparation:
1. Fold back the husks over the corn and remove the corn silk. Then place the ears of corn into water for 2–3 hours.
2. Drain the ears of corn, add salt and pepper, wrap a slice of bacon around each, and then fold back the husks around the ear again. Tie with a piece of butcher's string at the top, so that they hold together better.
3. Smoke at 230° Fahrenheit [110°C] for 1 ½ hours, then fold back the husks again, butter the ears of corn and serve hot.

Cinnamon Squash

This recipe is ideal for ushering in the transition from autumn to winter. It is best prepared with a butternut squash. You can alternatively use a small Hokkaido squash.

Ingredients:	1		medium-sized butternut squash
	1	tsp.	olive oil
	6	tbsp.	butter
	2	tsp.	brown sugar
	1	tsp.	cinnamon
	½	tsp.	chili flakes

Preparation:
1. Halve the squash and rub with the oil all around. In the process, do not yet remove the seeds.
2. With the cut side down place in the smoker and smoke at 230° Fahrenheit [110°C] for two hours.
3. In the meantime melt the butter, stir in the remaining ingredients, and keep everything warm.
4. Once cooked, remove the squash halves from the smoker, deseed, and cut into quarters. Brush with the cinnamon butter and serve hot.

BBQ'd Rice

Rice from the smoker? Why not? Whether it's with vegetables, spices, or plain, it is always a welcome and easy-to-prepare side dish.

Ingredients:	1	cup	rice, uncooked
	1		carrot, cut into fine strips
	1	stalk	celery, cut into fine strips
	1		red pepper, finely diced
	1		onion, diced
	4	tbsp.	butter
	2	cups	chicken or vegetable broth

Preparation:
1. In a baking dish combine the rice and vegetables and add the broth.
2. Spread clumps of butter on top and cover the dish with aluminum foil.
3. Place into the smoker and cook at 230° Fahrenheit [110°C] for 1½ hours until almost all liquid from the rice has been absorbed.
4. Remove the aluminum foil and smoke the rice once more for 20 minutes.
5. Either serve immediately or cover with aluminum foil and keep warm.

BREAD

Bread was and remains the ideal companion for meals. Whether it's a traditional cornbread from the South or a French baguette, much is possible in a smoker. The most important requirement is the necessary high heat of 356°–392° Fahrenheit [180°C–200°C] during baking.

Many types of smokers, for example the bullet or offset smoker, are heated up very well from relighting and thus bread baking is also possible in the pit. The side firebox on the offset smoker is very useful because you can use the already higher temperatures well for baking, and you do not have to heat up the entire smoker. The charcoal in the side firebox is then pushed together on one side, and the baked goods are placed on the opposite side.

Apple-Squash Bread

Thickly spread with butter or marmalade and together with a cup of tea or coffee—this bread is a tasty companion in autumn.

Ingredients:	½		butternut or Hokkaido squash, pureed
	1		apple, pureed
	2	cups	flour
	1	cup	apple juice
	2		eggs
	¾	cup	brown sugar
	¼	cup	olive oil
	1	packet	baking powder
	½	tsp.	salt
	½	tsp.	nutmeg
	1	tsp.	cinnamon

Preparation:

1. Heat the apple juice in a pot, reduce to half, and let cool.
2. Add the squash and apple puree, eggs, sugar, and oil to the apple juice and thoroughly mix.
3. Combine the dry ingredients in a mixing bowl and then combine with the puree mixture to form a smooth dough.
4. Then move the charcoal in the side firebox to one side so that you have space for baking, or heat the smoker to 356° Fahrenheit [180°C].
5. Fill the dough into a loaf pan and bake for approximately one hour until a wooden pick inserted in the bread comes out dry.

Corn Bread

This traditional recipe cannot be ignored—and when you try it for the first time you'll soon decide it belongs in your regular home diet.

Ingredients:	1	cup	flour
	1	cup	cornmeal
	1	cup	buttermilk
	2		eggs
	½	cup	sugar
	½	tsp.	baking soda
	½	tsp.	salt
	3½	oz.	butter, melted

Preparation:

1. Melt the butter in a pot, remove from the flame, and stir in the sugar. Add the eggs and mix well with a whisk.
2. Add the buttermilk and baking soda, stir in the dry ingredients one by one, and mix well.
3. Then move the charcoal in the side firebox to one side so that you have space for baking, or heat the smoker to 356° Fahrenheit [180°C].
4. Fill the dough into a correspondingly large, heat-resistant, greased baking dish and bake for 30–40 minutes until a wood pick inserted in the bread comes out dry.

Cheesy Corn Bread

Two types of cheese and green chilies make this bread especially spicy. You can easily do without butter or another topping because everything is already inside. In addition, creamed corn is in the dough, an ingredient that you do not have to buy but that is quick to prepare yourself.

Ingredients: Dough

1	cup	flour
1	cup	cornmeal
½	cup	cheddar, grated
½	cup	Fontina or Gruyère, grated
3½	oz.	jar of chili peppers, drained and finely chopped
½	lb.	butter, melted
4		eggs
1	cup	sugar
4	tsp.	baking powder
½	tsp.	salt

Creamed Corn

2	tbsp.	butter, melted
1	cup	milk
1	tbsp.	flour
½	tsp.	salt
14	oz.	canned corn

Preparation:
1. For the creamed corn, stir flour and salt into the melted butter. Add milk and constantly stir until a thick consistency is formed. Then stir in the corn, cook for approximately five more minutes, and then let cool.
2. Beat the butter and sugar until frothy and stir in the eggs one by one. Then fold in the chili peppers, cheese, and creamed corn.
3. In a mixing bowl combine the dry ingredients and then mix with the corn mixture until there are no longer any small clumps.
4. Then move the charcoal in the side firebox to one side so that you have space for baking, or heat the smoker to 302° Fahrenheit [150°C].
5. Fill the dough into a correspondingly large, heat-resistant, greased baking dish and bake for approximately one hour until a wood pick inserted in the bread comes out dry.

Mediterranean Rolls

With a few extra ingredients, this simple yeast dough becomes something special. Of course nut, vegetable, or herb breads are made in the same way. For a hot version, chorizo and chili peppers, for example, are well suited additions.

Ingredients:

1	lb.	flour
1	cup	water, lukewarm
1	cube	yeast
2	tbsp.	olive oil
1	tsp.	sugar
1	tsp.	coarse salt
¼	cup	sun-dried tomatoes, diced
¼	cup	arugula, chopped
¼	cup	black olives, chopped
1		chili pepper

Preparation:
1. Mix the sun-dried tomatoes, arugula, olives, and chili pepper (with or without seeds, according to taste).
2. Dissolve the yeast in the water while adding oil, sugar, and salt.
3. Then sift in the flour and slowly work to form an elastic dough, in the process kneading in the tomato mixture.
4. Separate the dough into eight even portions and leave covered for 15 minutes.
5. Meanwhile move the charcoal in the side firebox to one side so that you have space for baking, or heat the smoker to 392° Fahrenheit [200°C].
6. Bake on a baking stone or a floured sheet for 15–20 minutes.

Pecan Banana Bread

This bread is known for its sweetness; it is also very rich. The bananas provide the moistness, the nuts make the bread crunchy. Walnuts can alternately be used here.

Ingredients:	2	cups	flour
	1½	tsp.	baking powder
	½	tsp.	baking soda
	3	oz.	butter, soft
	1	tsp.	salt
	2		eggs
	½	cup	sugar
	3	tbsp.	milk
	1		banana, mashed
	½	cup	pecans, chopped

Preparation:
1. Thoroughly mix the nuts and the dry ingredients, except for the sugar, and set aside.
2. In a mixing bowl whip the sugar and butter and add the eggs one by one and milk. In the process continue beating.
3. Add the flour mixture and the bananas and mix to form a smooth dough. Then fold in the nuts.
4. Move the charcoal in the side firebox to one side so that you have space for baking, or heat the smoker to 356° Fahrenheit [180°C].
5. Fill the dough into a correspondingly large, heat-resistant, greased baking dish and bake for approximately one hour until a wood pick inserted in the bread comes out dry.
6. Let sit for ten minutes in the dish, then carefully turn upside down and let cool.

Zucchini Bread

At first glance the ingredients for this dough are somewhat unusual. But the zucchini just makes this bread moist; the unusual flavor comes from the vanilla and cinnamon.

Ingredients:	3	cups	flour
	3		eggs
	2	cups	sugar
	1		medium-sized zucchini, grated
	1	cup	vegetable oil
	1	tsp.	salt
	1	tsp.	baking soda
	1	tsp.	baking powder
	3	tsp.	cinnamon
	1½	tbsp.	vanilla flavoring
	1	cup	walnuts, chopped

Preparation:
1. In a mixing bowl, mix the flour, salt, baking powder, baking soda, and cinnamon and set aside.
2. In a second bowl beat the eggs with the sugar until frothy and add the oil and vanilla. Add the flour mixture and stir to form a smooth dough.
3. In the meantime, move the charcoal in the side firebox to one side so that you have space for baking, or heat the smoker to 392° Fahrenheit [200°C].
4. Fold in the zucchini and nuts, and fill the dough into a correspondingly large, heat-resistant, greased baking dish and bake for approximately 40–50 minutes until a wood pick inserted in the bread comes out dry.
5. Let sit in the dish for ten minutes, then carefully turn upside down and let cool.

Baguette

Voilá! The typical French bread is perfect for absorbing the juice from a nice steak. The secret is the rise time, the special type of flour, and the shape.

Ingredients: 2½   cups   flour, type 550
               1   tsp.   sugar
               ½   cube   yeast
               1   tsp.   salt
               1½   cups   water, lukewarm

Preparation: 1.   Mix the salt and flour in a mixing bowl and make a depression in the center.
               2.   Pour half of the water into the depression, crumble in the yeast, and add the sugar. Dissolve the yeast in the water and let sit covered for 30 minutes.
               3.   Then add the remaining water and form a dough ball, kneading well at least ten minutes in the process.
               4.   Let sit covered for two hours, knead again, and let sit for two hours once again.
               5.   Separate the dough into three parts and roll out each piece to form a thin rectangle. Then roll up from the wide side, cut into the top side 3–4 times diagonally, and let rest for 30 minutes on a floured sheet.
               6.   Meanwhile move the charcoal in the side firebox to one side so that you have space for baking, or heat the smoker to 392° Fahrenheit [200°C].
               7.   Brush the baguettes with some salt water and bake for 20–25 minutes on a baking stone or the floured sheet. The baguettes should be golden brown.

SNACKS

Most of the dishes prepared in the smoker are quick and easy to make, but the cooking process is very time-consuming. So that you survive this time without hunger pangs, you should use the heat of the smoker for small snacks and appetizers.

Moink Balls

Moo + oink = moink. Beef and pork united in the form of ground meat and bacon.

Traditionally moink balls were made from finished, precooked meatballs, but here fresh ground beef is used.

Ingredients:

Rub

2	tbsp.	paprika powder
1	tbsp.	black pepper, freshly ground
½	tsp.	chili powder
½	tsp.	onion powder
½	tsp.	garlic powder
2	tsp.	celery salt
1	pinch	cayenne pepper

Meat

2	lbs.	ground beef
12	slices	bacon

Glaze

1	cup	ketchup or BBQ according to taste
3	tbsp.	honey
1	tsp.	Tabasco sauce

Additional

24		**small wood skewers or toothpicks**

Preparation:

1. Mix the ingredients for the rub and then add to the ground beef, mix thoroughly and knead until it begins to stick to your hands.
2. From the ground meat form 24 equally large balls at approximately 1½ oz.
3. Halve the bacon slices crosswise, wrap the balls in a half slice each, and fix with a small wood skewer.
4. Place in the smoker for 45 minutes. In the meantime, mix the glaze.
5. Brush the moink balls with the glaze and smoke for an additional ten minutes.
6. Leave the wood skewer in the meat when serving, thus you can conveniently enjoy the moink balls as a snack.

Armadillo Eggs

For this BBQ classic habaneros or jalapeños are concealed in the ground meat, which is hellishly hot but just as delicious.

Ingredients:

½	tsp.	cumin
1	tsp.	salt
1	tsp.	black pepper, freshly ground
1	tbsp.	paprika powder
1	tbsp.	Worcester sauce
1		onion, finely diced
2		garlic cloves, finely minced
1		egg

Meat

2	lbs.	ground beef

Stuffing

6		habaneros or jalapeños, hotness according to taste
7	oz.	cheddar, finely diced

Glaze
BBQ sauce according to taste

Preparation:

1. Fill the habaneros with cheddar. In case there is extra, add to the remaining ingredients.
2. Mix all remaining ingredients with the ground meat and knead until it sticks on your hands.
3. Divide the ground meat mixture into six evenly large pieces, wrap the habaneros well in it, and shape into eggs.
4. Smoke for five minutes, coat with BBQ sauce, and cook another 20 minutes.
5. Serve hot and keep enough milk nearby for "extinguishing."

A.B.T.'s

Written out, these extremely hot snacks are called "atomic buffalo turds." But they taste much better than the name implies...

Ingredients:
20		jalapeños
20		smokies
½	lb.	cream cheese
20	slices	bacon
1	tbsp.	brown sugar
¼		onion, finely diced

Additional
Several toothpicks

Preparation:
1. Cut off the stems of the jalapeños. Then halve, remove all seeds and veins, and keep together in pairs.
2. Stir together the sugar, onion, and cream cheese thoroughly, fill into a freezer bag, and cut off a corner of the bag.
3. With this pastry bag fill the mixture into the jalapeno halves, press a smokie into each pepper, and fold together. Make sure that the halves fit together.
4. Wrap a slice of bacon around each jalapeno and fix with toothpicks.
5. Smoke for two hours and serve hot.

Steaks

Simple, quick, plain, and basically good. A high-quality steak is honest meat and for its preparation you will basically only need pepper, salt, and heat. Here a little fennel seed is added. The side firebox with wood fire or live charcoal can serve as a source of heat.

Ingredients:

Rub
1	tbsp.	black peppercorns
½	tbsp.	fennel seed

Meat
2	Rib eye, t-bone, or rump steaks, 1–1½" thick

Additional
olive oil
Fleur de Sel

Preparation:
1. Cook the peppercorn and fennel seed in an ungreased pan until they are fragrant. Then thoroughly crush in a mortar.
2. Lightly oil the steaks and rub with the rub all around. Set aside so that they get to room temperature.
3. Grill over direct heat on each side for three minutes.
4. Place into the smoker and slowly bring to a core temperature of 135° Fahrenheit [57°C]. Monitor this step with a probe thermometer.
5. Remove from the smoker, wrap in aluminum foil, and let rest for five minutes.
6. Cut into slices, sprinkle with *fleur de sel*, and serve.

Burgers

The heat in the side firebox is ideal for grilling a couple of burgers, in the meantime. This recipe is classically prepared with bacon and cheese.

Ingredients:	Seasoning Mix		
	1	cup	onions, finely diced
	1	tsp.	garlic, finely minced
	1	tsp.	thyme
	1	tsp.	Worcester sauce
	½	tsp.	salt
	½	tsp.	black pepper, ground
	½	tsp.	Tabasco sauce
	Meat		
	1¼	lbs.	ground beef
	4	slices	bacon
	Additional		
	4	slices	cheese (such as gouda or edam cheese)
	4		hamburger buns
			hamburger sauce
			ketchup or BBQ sauce according to taste
	1–2		tomatoes
	½		iceberg lettuce

Preparation:
1. Render the bacon in a pan, drain on a paper towel, and finely chop.
2. Cook the onion for approximately five minutes in the bacon fat until soft. Add the garlic and thyme and continue cooking for two more minutes. Let cool.
3. Mix well with the ground beef and knead until the mixture begins to stick. Then form four burgers.
4. Directly grill each side for four minutes, in the last minute place cheese on top of the burgers.
5. Dress the burgers on the hamburger rolls according to preference with lettuce, tomatoes, etc., and serve immediately.

Smoked Raclette

Here a Swiss national dish is prepared in an American manner. Instead of bread or potatoes for dipping, you can of course also use any type of vegetables. If you like it spicier, use Gruyère or Bergkäse.

Ingredients:	12	oz.	raclette cheese in one piece
	1	tbsp.	coarse Dijon mustard
	1	tbsp.	sherry
			salt and pepper to season, to taste
			jacket potatoes or bread for dipping

Preparation:
1. Spread the cheese in a small baking dish and brush with mustard.
2. Place the dish into the smoker and smoke for 1½ hours.
3. Remove from the smoker, mix in the sherry, and season with salt and pepper according to taste.
4. Serve hot and dip with bread or pour over the potatoes.

Smoked Nuts

These nuts taste good for a light snack or cooled down as a snack for TV night. If packaged airtight in a can, they can be stored for 2–3 weeks.

Ingredients:	½	cup	brown sugar
	1	tsp.	rosemary, dried
	1	tsp.	thyme, dried
	1	pinch	cayenne pepper
	1	pinch	mustard powder
	1½	cups	mixed salted nuts
	3	tbsp.	olive oil

Preparation:
1. Mix all ingredients in a freezer bag.
2. Place a correspondingly large sheet of aluminum foil or a griddle in the smoker and spread out the nuts in a layer on it.
3. Smoke for one hour, mixing every now and then.
4. Either serve hot immediately or cooled later.

Kansas City Buffalo Wings

Because of their small size, buffalo wings are cooked in a short period of time and you will quickly have something delicious to nibble on. The sweet rub goes very well with a hot BBQ sauce.

Ingredients:	Finger-Lickin' Rub		
	1	cup	brown sugar
	½	cup	paprika powder, sweet
	2½	tbsp.	black pepper, freshly ground
	2½	tbsp.	coarse salt
	1½	tbsp.	chili powder
	1½	tbsp.	onion powder
	1–2	tsp.	cayenne pepper

Meat

| | 2 | lbs. | chicken wings |

Glaze
Hot BBQ sauce

Preparation:
1. The day before barbecuing, mix all ingredients for the rub and rub the chicken wings all over with it. Let marinate overnight in the refrigerator.
2. The next day place the wings in the smoker and smoke for two hours, in the process glaze with BBQ sauce according to taste after one hour.
3. Serve hot with additional sauce.

Shellfish Skewers

Water chestnuts, that are skewered together with the shellfish, are in every Asian shop.

Ingredients:	Shellfish Marinade		
	¼	cup	sake (rice wine)
	2	tsp.	brown sugar
	2	tsp.	peanut oil

Skewers

	1	can	water chestnuts, drained
	4		scallions, cut into 3/4" long pieces
	1	lb.	scallop meat, without coral

Additional
bamboo skewers

Preparation:
1. Mix the marinade ingredients and let the shellfish marinate in it for 30 minutes.
2. Alternating, stick water chestnuts, scallions, and shellfish on the bamboo skewers and place in the smoker.
3. Smoke for 15–20 minutes, the shellfish should still be slightly translucent in the center.

DESSERTS

Dessert is the culmination of a good meal. And because the smoker is at temperature anyway, it is ideal for preparing dessert.

Classics such as cobbler and crisp must be present. They belong to dessert culture like pulled pork belongs to BBQ.

The main difference from the customary smoker operation is the higher pit temperature of 320°– 392° Fahrenheit [160°C–200°C] required for most desserts. With most types of smokers, like the bullet or offset smoker, the temperature is quickly raised by relighting, thus baking in the pit is a breeze. Specifically with offset smokers the side firebox also plays a useful role because you can use the already higher temperature well for baking and do not have to heat up the entire smoker. The charcoal in the side firebox is then moved to one side and the dessert has its place on the other "cooler" side.

Smoked Baked Bananas

First the sweet bananas get some spicy smoke and are then cooked until they are soft and creamy.

Ingredients:

4		bananas
4	sprigs	rosemary
4	tsp.	honey or maple syrup
4	tbsp.	walnuts, chopped

Preparation:

1. Halve the unpeeled bananas lengthwise and place in the 230° Fahrenheit [110°C] hot smoker. Smoke for 20 minutes, in the process place the rosemary sprigs in the charcoal.
2. Then move the charcoal in the side firebox to one side so that you have space for baking, or heat the smoker to 392° Fahrenheit [200°C].
3. Remove the bananas from their peels and place into a heat-resistant and correspondingly big bowl.
4. Spread honey or syrup and nuts onto the banana halves and bake for 20 minutes in the smoker until the bananas are soft and golden yellow.

Peach Cobbler

Cobbler is a cake, mostly with fruit, that has two variations. In this version, the fruit is placed into a thin dough in which it sinks. The dough raises during baking and surrounds the fruit.

Ingredients:
Dough

2	cups	flour
1	tsp.	baking powder
1	tsp.	salt
3		eggs
½	lb.	butter
½	cup	*crème frâiche*
3–4	drops	vanilla flavoring
½	tsp.	cinnamon

Filling

2		peaches, peeled and cut into wedges
1	pinch	nutmeg
		powdered sugar

Preparation:

1. Move the charcoal in the side firebox to one side so that you have space for baking, or heat the smoker to 356° Fahrenheit [180°C].
2. Grease a baking dish and sprinkle with flour.
3. Thoroughly mix the ingredients for the dough, stir until smooth, and pour into the dish.
4. Spread the peach wedges on top and sprinkle with nutmeg.
5. Bake for 35–40 minutes and sprinkle with powdered sugar before serving.

Fruit Cobbler

For this second cobbler version, the fruit first goes into the dish and is then covered with dough. You can use any fruit here, whatever is in season and available.

Ingredients:
Dough

1	cup	flour
½	cup	sugar
1	tsp.	salt
2	tsp.	baking powder
1½	cups	buttermilk
5	oz.	butter, melted

Fruit

3	cups	seasonal fruit

Filling

½	cup	water
4	tbsp.	brown sugar
1	tbsp.	starch
1	tbsp	lemon juice

Preparation:

1. Move the charcoal in the side firebox to one side so that you have space for baking, or heat the smoker to 356° Fahrenheit [180°C].
2. Cut the fruit into bite-sized pieces and spread in a greased baking dish.
3. Mix the ingredients for the filling, bring to a boil, and pour over the fruit.
4. For the dough, first mix the dry ingredients, then stir in the butter and buttermilk, and smoothly spread the dough onto the fruit.
5. Bake for 50 minutes and serve warm.

Pecan Pie

Pecan pie also belongs among the traditional recipes. If you cannot get pecans, walnuts are a good alternative.

Ingredients:			
	1	cup	brown sugar
	½	cup	sugar beet syrup
	4	tbsp.	butter
	3	tbsp.	rum
	4	drops	vanilla flavoring
	½	tsp.	salt
	4		eggs
	2	tbsp.	cream
	2	cups	pecans or walnuts
	1		flan case

Preparation:
1. Move the charcoal in the side firebox to one side so that you have space for baking, or heat the smoker to 356° Fahrenheit [180°C].
2. Mix the sugar, syrup, butter, rum, vanilla flavoring, and salt, cook for one minute, and then let the mixture cool.
3. Beat the eggs with the cream and combine well with the cooled mixture.
4. Fold in the nuts and spread the mixture on the flan case. Garnish with a few nuts.
5. Bake for 40–50 minutes and serve warm.

Apple Crisp

The word crisp refers to the topping that resembles streusel. With a scoop of vanilla ice cream, this dessert is a true temptation. Like so many apples in history...

Ingredients:	Topping		
	1	cup	oats
	2	tbsp.	flour
	½	cup	brown sugar
	½	cup	butter, melted
	Filling		
	6		apples, peeled, cut into thin wedges
	¼	cup	brown sugar
	¼	cup	orange juice
	2	tsp.	starch
	1	tsp.	cinnamon

Preparation:
1. Move the charcoal in the side firebox to one side so that you have space for baking, or heat the smoker to 356° Fahrenheit [180°C].
2. Mix the ingredients for the topping.
3. Then combine the filling for all ingredients and pour into a baking dish.
4. Sprinkle the topping, bake for 45 minutes, and serve warm.

Baked Half Skin Apple

This baked apple brings its own plate because only half of it is peeled. You can spoon it from the bottom peel half. The apple is best peeled off when you carve it in the center all around beforehand. To do this, hold the knife at the front on the edge and turn the apple on the table along the point of the knife.

Ingredients: Filling

¼	cup	apricot jam
¼	cup	raisins
3	tbsp.	calvados
½	tsp.	allspice (ground)
1	pinch	cardamom
4	tsp.	butter
2	oz.	marzipan paste
6	tbsp.	almonds, sliced

Apples

4		red apples (such as Braeburn)
1		lemon or lime

Topping

4	tbsp.	double cream 42%
4	tbsp.	maple syrup
1	tbsp.	calvados
2	tbsp.	chopped pistachios
		powdered sugar and cinnamon

Preparation:
1. Move the charcoal in the side firebox to one side so that you have space for baking, or heat the smoker to 356° Fahrenheit [180°C].
2. Place the apples with the stems down and then remove the core on the other side. Do not cut in too deep, as a base should remain.
3. With a knife, carve the peel of the apple horizontally in the center all around and peel the top side, opposite the stem side. Immediately brush all of the cut surfaces with lemon juice so that they do not become brown.
4. Completely roast the almonds and place half aside.
5. Mix the other half of the almonds with the remaining ingredients except for the butter until the marzipan has almost dissolved. Fill the mixture into the apples and place a teaspoon of butter on the opening of each.
6. Wrap individual apples in aluminum foil, seal as tight as possible, and cook for 30 minutes. Carefully remove from the foil, place on a plate, and pour the juice from the foil on top.
7. Mix the double cream, maple syrup, and calvados, season to taste, and pour one tablespoon on each apple.
8. Sprinkle with the remaining almonds and garnish with powdered sugar, cinnamon, and pistachios.

Rhubarb Crunch

Rhubarb, with its sweet and sour taste, is always an excellent ingredient for desserts with which you can surprise and indulge your guests.

Ingredients:

1	cup	flour
1	cup	oats
1	cup	brown sugar
½	cup	butter, melted
1	tsp.	anise, ground
1	tsp.	cinnamon
3½	cups	rhubarb pieces, approximately ¾" long
1	tbsp.	starch
4	drops	vanilla flavoring
½	cup	water

Preparation:
1. Move the charcoal in the side firebox to one side so that you have space for baking, or heat the smoker to 356° Fahrenheit [180°C].
2. Mix the flour, oats, butter, cinnamon, anise, and half of the sugar, firmly press half of the mixture onto the bottom of a baking dish.
3. Cover evenly with the rhubarb pieces.
4. Mix the other half of the sugar with the starch and water in a pot and simmer for 3–5 minutes with constant stirring until the liquid is clear. Then stir in the vanilla flavoring.
5. Spread the sauce over the rhubarb and sprinkle with the second half of the oat mixture.
6. Bake for approximately one hour, until the top is crispy and serve warm.

Cinnamon Rolls

Because these cinnamon rolls are made from a yeast dough, you should make sure that the dough can rise over a sufficiently long period of time.

Ingredients:
Dough

2	oz.	butter, liquid
1¼	cups	lukewarm milk
1		egg
1	tbsp.	sugar
½	tsp.	salt
1	packet	vanilla pudding powder
18	oz.	flour
1	packet	dry yeast

Filling

3	oz.	soft butter
½	cup	brown sugar
2	tsp.	cinnamon
½	cup	pecans, chopped

Additional

½	cup	hazelnut brittle
		vanilla sauce

Preparation:

1. Mix the ingredients for the dough and knead until an elastic yeast dough develops. Cover the mixing bowl with a damp kitchen towel and let the dough rise for one hour.
2. Roll the dough out into a large rectangle, brush with butter, sprinkle the remaining ingredients of the filling on top, and roll up from the wide side.
3. Cut the roll into 1" thick slices (rolls) and place into a correspondingly large, greased baking dish. Leave ¼"–¾" space between the rolls.
4. Cover the rolls with a damp kitchen towel and let rise for one hour until they have risen where they are touching each other.
5. Meanwhile move the charcoal in the side firebox to one side so that you have space for baking, or heat the smoker to 392° Fahrenheit [200°C].
6. Bake the cinnamon rolls for approximately 15–20 minutes and serve warm with vanilla sauce and brittle.

Emma's Fabulous Nut Wedges

As a dessert, snack, or food for traveling, these nut wedges are simply unbeatable. Just like the inventor of this recipe...

Ingredients: Dough

1¼	cups	flour
5	oz.	butter
⅓	cup	sugar
1		egg

Topping

1	cup	apricot marmalade
1½	cups	hazelnuts, coarsely grated
5	oz.	butter
1¼	cups	sugar
4	tbsp.	water

Additional

1	pack	couverture

Preparation:

1. Mix the dough ingredients, thoroughly knead until a smooth dough is formed, and roll out on one, possibly two, correspondingly large baking sheets and poke with a fork.
2. Spread the apricot marmalade on the dough.
3. Then bring butter, sugar, and water to a boil, add the nuts, and briefly cook together. Let cool slightly.
4. Distribute the mixture evenly over the dough and carefully spread. In the process the marmalade should remain underneath the mixture.
5. In the meantime, move the charcoal in the side firebox to one side so that you have space for baking, or heat the smoker to 392° Fahrenheit [200°C].
6. Bake for 20–30 minutes, until the desired browning is reached.
7. Cut the nut wedges into triangles immediately after baking and let cool. Then melt the couverture in a double boiler and dip the corners in the chocolate.

Part 3:
APPENDIX

Glossary

Baby back ribs:
Also called loin ribs or back ribs.
The first 4" of the back rib cage.

Barrel smoker:
Also called offset smoker.

Baste:
Another term for a mop sauce.

Brine:
A solution whose tartness makes
the meat tender. It may be lactic
acid, fruit acid, or also brine.

Bullet smoker:
Also called water smoker.

Charcoal grate:
Grate on which charcoal or
wood is placed in the smoker so
that oxygen comes from below.

Charcoal starter:
Tool for grilling that quickly and
easily lights the charcoal in a
container.

Chunks:
Larger (approximately 1 1/2"
x 1 1/2") pieces of wood for
smoking.

Coral:
The roe of the scallop.

Fleur de sel:
Also called "flower" of salt.
Topmost layer on the water
surface, coarse and flavorful
salt.

Injection:
Injection fluid that is injected
with a thick injection needle.

Jerk:
Jamaican term for BBQ.

Loin ribs:
Another term for baby back ribs

Minion method:
Method of setting up charcoal
at long BBQs named after Jim
Minion.

Mop:
Mop brush that can absorb a lot of sauce.

Mop sauce:
Thin sauce that flavors and keeps the meat juicy.

Offset smoker:
See barrel smoker.

Paste:
A rub with fresh or liquid ingredients.

Pit:
Term for the cooking area in the smoker.

Pit master:
Term for the person who stands at the smoker, also at the pit (cooking area).

PP: Abbreviation for pulled pork.

Pulled pork:
Shredded pork.

Reduce:
Technical term for boiling down.

Rub:
A dry mixture of spices.

SFB:
Abbreviation for side firebox.

St. Louis Cut:
Spare ribs, special type of rib cut, underneath the baby back ribs.

Stack:
A module ring in water smokers.

Water smoker:
Water or bullet smoker.

Wood chips:
Wooden chips for smoking.

Notes on the Recipes

Conversions

Here you will find the exact conversion values:

Liquid Volume in the Kitchen:

1 cup	=	16 tablespoons	=	236.6 ml.
1 tablespoon	=	3 teaspoons	=	14.79 ml.
1 teaspoon	=			4.929 ml.

In stores you will find very practical measuring instruments with which you can measure precise amounts. If you would rather make do with normal utensils, simply use heaped tablespoons and teaspoons.

Flour and Powdered Sugar

$\frac{1}{8}$	cup	=	15	Grams
$\frac{1}{4}$	cup	=	30	Grams
$\frac{1}{3}$	cup	=	40	Grams
$\frac{3}{8}$	cup	=	45	Grams
$\frac{1}{2}$	cup	=	60	Grams
$\frac{2}{3}$	cup	=	75	Grams
$\frac{3}{4}$	cup	=	85	Grams
1	cup	=	120	Grams

Butter and Sugar

$\frac{1}{8}$	cup	=	30	Grams
$\frac{1}{4}$	cup	=	55	Grams
$\frac{1}{3}$	cup	=	75	Grams
$\frac{3}{8}$	cup	=	85	Grams
$\frac{1}{2}$	cup	=	115	Grams
$\frac{2}{3}$	cup	=	150	Grams
$\frac{3}{4}$	cup	=	170	Grams
1	cup	=	225	Grams

Lighting a smoker for small amounts is hardly worthwhile. Therefore, mostly larger amounts of meat, fish, or poultry are prepared in it. For this reason, and because a successful smoker day lasts for many hours and you actually continually eat, we have done without an exact number of people for the recipes.

If you use the rule of thumb, 7 oz. of meat for a "normal" eater plus side dishes, you can easily increase or decrease the quantities according to personal preferences.

Notes on the Recipes

If you do not want to make the BBQ sauces yourself, here are our shopping tips:

Particularly in the United States shoppers stand before long shelves with hundreds of different BBQ sauces, and the choice is not easy. All flavors are available—only trying them out helps.

In Germany the selection is manageable, and the main criterion for your purchase should be to choose BBQ sauces without artificial flavors and preservatives, which are also offered from several manufacturers.

We recommend the Bone Suckin' sauces from the United States that are also easily obtained in Germany. If you prefer a somewhat stronger BBQ flavor, you should get the Dinosaur sauces. If you really want to fire up yourself and your guests, do not pass on the HotMamas sauces. They are made in Germany and distinguish themselves with their outstanding quality.

The classic sauce, HP, from England, next to the popular Stubb's sauces, should also be mentioned.

We, the German Grilling Sports Club, will also take on sauces and starting in 2011 bring our own BBQ sauces to the market.

Recipes from A to Z

Recipes from A to Z

Index

D

Digital probe thermometer, 42
Digital thermometer, 42
Direct grill, 25
Drain, 31

E

Enamel, 31

F

Farmer, 6, 22 ff.
Fire, 38
Firebed, 17
Fleur de Sel, 138

G

Glaze, 47, 69, 138
Grate lifter, 42
Grill brush with scraper, 42
Grill tongs, 42

H

Handles, 25, 31
Heat, 16, 26, 30, 34
Heat buffer, 26
Hickory, 29, 35

I

Injection, 138
Inlet dampers, 23

J

Joe's, 6, 23

K

Kamado, 30
Kettle grill, 29
Kindling, 38
Knife, 43

L

Lid, 22 ff., 31, 38, 64
Light, 36
Linseed oil-graphite-turpentine substitute mixture, 31
Loin ribs, 138
Louisiana, 6, 29
Low and slow, 11
Low temperature, 11, 17, 19, 97

M

Maintenance, 20 ff., 31
Material thickness, 23, 31
Meat hook, 42
Mesquite, 29, 35
Minion method, 28
Mop, 54, 139
Mop sauce, 139
Mop with bucket, 42

N

Napoleon, 6, 27
Neck, 19, 63, 64
North Carolina, 18

O

Oak, 35
Offset smoker, 22 f., 139

P

Paste, 52, 139
Pig pits, 18
Pit, 17, 22, 24, 25, 139
Pit master, 17, 34, 139
PP, 139
Pulled pork, 18, 64, 139
Pulling, 17, 64

Index